Twayne's United States Authors Series

Sylvia E. Bowman, *Editor*

INDIANA UNIVERSITY

Paul Elmer More

PAUL ELMER MORE

by FRANCIS X. DUGGAN

University of Santa Clara

 106

Twayne Publishers, Inc.   ::   New York

FOR
BART J. DUGGAN

Preface

CRITICISM has for some time been a distinctive category of American literature. Its dependence upon the primary genres and the related fact of its not being in itself a re-creation of primary experience will keep it from becoming what the novel became in nineteenth-century England and Russia or what the drama became in Elizabethan England; but criticism has been practiced in the United States in the twentieth century on an unprecedented scale. Critics have heretofore usually been something else besides, and that something else has usually taken their major effort; one of the peculiarities of recent American literature is the sizeable body of writers for whom criticism has been a life's work. Among the first of these, in achievement as well as in time, is Paul Elmer More. He is not, let me add immediately, so important a critic as others we might name; his criticism has not changed our conception of what literature is, as the criticism of Coleridge or of T. S. Eliot has. More is a critic of another sort; like Lewis Mumford or F. O. Matthiessen, he reads the literature of the past to see what it means to him and to his age, and in doing so discovers new meanings for us all.

More, who thought himself "at once the least read and the worst hated author in the country,"[1] is even less read, if less hated, today. Except in anthologies, his literary essays have until recently long been out of print; and even in anthologies he is less often represented than his friend Irving Babbitt, despite the fact that Babbitt was less concerned with literary values. Yet H. L. Mencken, antagonist of More though he was, admitted during More's lifetime that he was "the nearest approach to a genuine scholar that we have in America, God save us all!"[2] And one of More's reviewers described the *Shelburne Essays* as covering "a larger range of subjects competently treated than any other living American critic can exhibit"[3]—a statement which needs no modification today.

When the first volume of *Shelburne Essays* appeared in 1904,[4] American criticism was dominated by the genteel school of Edmund C. Stedman, George E. Woodberry, Hamilton Wright Mabie, Henry van Dyke, Barrett Wendell, and others—a school which had long been under attack by the realists and which was soon to be displaced. Since More was then nearly forty and a prolific writer—six more volumes of *Shelburne Essays* came out in the next six years, and several periodicals were regularly carrying his articles and reviews—he might have been expected to make his strongest impression on his age by the time of World War I. He was well known before the war, and widely respected too; but his strongest impact came toward the end of the 1920's.

The reason is easy to see. More found so little to interest him in contemporary literature that, except for an infrequent scornful reference to "our mutually admiring poets, whether imagist, symbolist, anthologist, *vers-libriste*, or however else ticketed" (*SE*, X, x), the reader of his *Shelburne Essays* would hardly know such beings existed during the years of More's major critical activity. While other critics might tolerate or encourage what Mencken called the "goatishness" of the younger writers of the day[5] in the expectation that it would eventuate in something worthwhile, More believed that the characteristic literature of the twentieth century, which he collected under the heading of naturalism, must inevitably degenerate into "the clever futilities of an Aldous Huxley or the obscene rigmarole of a James Joyce, or, seeking to escape the curse of impotence, into the sadism of a Robinson Jeffers" (*NSE*, III, 15). Society and literature were better served by the critic who sought to preserve the best of the past and to impose it upon the present—by persuasion, example, and imaginative appeal if possible, or by constraint if necessary. The function of the college is not "to develope 'creative genius,'" but "to create a critical atmosphere which will keep the genius from going crazy."[6] It is something of a curiosity that although even in his social criticism More considered himself a "mere man of letters" (*SE*, VII, 171), his writings on contemporary affairs are nearly always on social or political questions. Not until the middle 1920's, when he was in his sixties, did he give any critical attention to the literature which we think of as peculiarly that of the twentieth century, and then he simply denounced it. On the other hand, the critics who came to prominence just before World War I and who far surpassed More in their popularity and influence owed their success to their participation in the exciting activity in the arts of drama, poetry, and fiction which began in America at about that time.

In short, More gave his energy to a criticism not then much in vogue while a group of younger men—notably Randolph Bourne, Van Wyck Brooks, and H. L. Mencken—encouraged a literature that dealt with the actual conditions of American life, whether or not those conditions met the requirements of an ethical ideal, and discouraged what they found in both the genteel tradition and Paul Elmer More: humility before European culture, the identification of American culture with New England, traditional moral idealism, and refusal to take contemporary literature seriously.

After Bourne, Brooks, and Mencken, criticism divided. Some critics, like Max Eastman, Lewis Mumford, V. F. Calverton, and Waldo Frank, stressed the social relevance of literature; others, like Joel Spingarn, Ezra Pound, T. S. Eliot, and the Fugitives, encouraged or practiced a formal analysis of literary texts; others brought to bear on literature the methods of a variety of disciplines. Not until late in the 1920's did the New Humanism of Babbitt and More, who were then supported by a group of younger critics, become a serious threat to the social realists and the formal critics. Some of the best known critics of the present time—Edmund Wilson, Kenneth Burke, Allen Tate, R. P. Blackmur, Malcolm Cowley, and Yvor Winters—took part in the New Humanist controversy that came to a head about 1930—about the time, incidentally, when More was twice considered for the Nobel Prize.[7]

The purpose of this book is to present an analysis and a criticism of the work of Paul Elmer More. Chapter One, a sketch of his early intellectual development, describes the philosophical motives and assumptions present in all his writings, social, literary, and philosophical. Chapter Two discusses the literary criticism of the *Shelburne Essays*. Chapter Three deals with More's social and political essays and with the environment in which he wrote them. Together, these chapters cover his career through the period of the *Shelburne Essays;* Chapters Four and Five cover his later career, although some overlapping is unavoidable. Chapter Four is a study of his work on Greek and Patristic philosophy and of his later intellectual and religious development. Chapter Five is a study of the literary criticism of the *New Shelburne Essays* and therefore of his engagement with the literary issues of the 1920's and 1930's. In the Conclusion I assess More's importance in American criticism.

I hardly need say that I am not competent to judge all aspects of More's work; my interest, as this Preface indicates, is chiefly in More's literary essays. But since in all his pronouncements on politics, economics, science, philosophy, and religion he spoke only as a man of letters and, despite his disclaimer, as a moralist (*SE*, VII, 171-72), I may without pretense—we are all moralists, are we not?—meet him on those grounds.

FRANCIS X. DUGGAN

University of Santa Clara

Acknowledgments

I acknowledge my obligation to a number of persons and institutions. My greatest debt is to Mr. A. H. Dakin, who has helped me for several years with information, encouragement, and advice, and whose criticism of the manuscript has saved me from many errors. Others are to Matthew J. Kelly, the Reverend John H. Gray, S.J., George J. Sullwold, and Joseph G. Dahms, who have read the manuscript in whole or in part. If any faults remain, I claim credit for them. My thanks also to the Reverend Charles A. Banet, C.PP.S., and the staff of the Library of Saint Joseph's College (Indiana); to the Reverend Edward R. A. Boland, S.J., and the staff of the Orradre Library, University of Santa Clara; and to the staffs of the Libraries of Princeton University, Stanford University, and San Jose State College. To Mrs. Harry B. Fine and Mrs. Edmund G. Dymond for permission to quote from their father's letters and from the *Shelburne Essays*. To the Princeton University Press, which holds copyright on the *New Shelburne Essays, The Greek Tradition,* and *Pages from an Oxford Diary*, for privileges extended through the Resolution on Permissions of the Association of American University Presses. To Mrs. Jack Wagnon, who typed the manuscript, and to Miss Sandra Pierotti and Miss Eloise M. Rosenblatt, who helped with proofreading. Finally, I offer thanks and apologies to my wife and children, who suffered at second hand (and hence compounded) the distresses of authorship.

Contents

Chronology

1864   Paul Elmer More born at St. Louis, Missouri, December 12, the fourth son and seventh of eight children of Enoch Anson and Katharine Hay (Elmer) More.

1883   Enters the College of Liberal Arts, Washington University.

1887   Graduates *cum laude*. Begins teaching at Smith Academy, St. Louis; continues there until 1892, except for the year 1888-1889.

1888-   First visit to Europe.
1889

1890   First book, *Helena and Occasional Poems*.

1891   Receives M.A. from Washington University.

1892   Enters Harvard for work in oriental and classical languages; meets Irving Babbitt.

1893   First scholarly article, "The Influences of Hindu Thought on Manichaeism." Receives M.A. from Harvard. Continues studies there till the spring of 1895, teaching Sanskrit as an assistant in 1894-1895; decides not to take a doctorate.

1895-   Teaches Sanskrit and classical literature at Bryn Mawr.
1897

1897-   Retires for study and meditation to Shelburne, New
1899   Hampshire, where he decides to make criticism and scholarship, rather than creative literature, his work. In 1898 he begins contributing literary essays to *Atlantic Monthly* and *New World*.

1900   Marries Henrietta Beck, of St. Louis; settles at East Orange, New Jersey.

1901   Joins *Independent,* primarily as literary editor.

1903   Resigns from *Independent* to become literary editor of New York *Evening Post*. Much of his work for *Evening Post* appears also in *Nation,* which is under the same ownership.

1904   First volume of *Shelburne Essays*.

1906 Becomes literary editor of *Nation* but maintains his position with *Evening Post.*

1909 Becomes editor of *Nation.*

1912 Spends summer in England.

1914 Resigns from *Nation* to begin a career of independent scholarship; makes his home at Princeton, New Jersey.

1915 *Aristocracy and Justice,* a collection of conservative political essays.

1917 *Platonism,* his first important book on Greek philosophy.

1919 Begins lecturing on Greek and Patristic philosophy at Princeton University. Elected to the American Academy of Arts and Letters.

1920-
1921 Edits the book section of *Unpartizan Review.*

1921 Concludes *Shelburne Essays* with the eleventh volume. Publishes *The Religion of Plato,* volume I of *The Greek Tradition.*

1924-
1925 Visits England; excursions to Italy and Greece. Out of this visit comes *Pages from an Oxford Diary,* published shortly after his death.

1926 Transfers from philosophy to classics at Princeton. Lectures on Plato and Greek philosophy at Harvard; teaches Greek at Radcliffe.

1928 *The Demon of the Absolute,* first volume of *New Shelburne Essays.* Mrs. More dies. More visits England.

1931 *The Catholic Faith,* concluding volume of *The Greek Tradition.*

1933 Spends summer in England.

1934 *The Sceptical Approach to Religion.*

1936 *On Being Human,* his last collection of literary essays.

1937 Dies, March 9.

Paul Elmer More

CHAPTER 1

Noetic Life

I *More's Early Religious Life*

PAUL ELMER MORE once sent to Robert Shafer, when Shafer was writing his *Paul Elmer More and American Criticism*,[1] a summary of what he called his "noetic life." The story is partly given in the reminiscent notes of "Marginalia," which More considered his closest approach to a public account of his "spiritual adventures and inner development"; as an anonymous diary in *Pages from an Oxford Diary;* in thin fictional disguise in his two early novels, *The Great Refusal* and *The Jessica Letters;* and elsewhere in piecemeal fashion—as in "Saint Augustine" (*SE*, VI, 65-66)—in his published writings.[2] The letter to Shafer, however, is the most concise of the various accounts, and for that reason I quote extensively from it:

> The key to understanding my essays—and I cannot blame those who do not possess it—is that my noetic life, if I may call it such, has been wrought out of separate strands which have appeared and reappeared in various combinations and antagonisms; so much so that to myself, when I dare to look back over the past, I seem to be not one but all mankind's epitome—not to mention Plato's many-headed beast. In my youth I was steeped in the rankest romantic literature of Germany, and suffered from it grievously, in ways that need not be described. Yet all the while there was a strong pull within me to the classics, at first the Latin and later the Greek. By the time I got to Harvard I had become acutely aware of the mischief done me, and had begun deliberately to refashion my taste on the classics. And in this B[abbitt], who was born in Horace's cradle, acted as a powerful stimulus. . . .

Another strand in this unstable compound was a hard, dry rationalism. While inditing tragedies and a huge epic in the romantic vein (fortunately long ago burnt), I was plotting out a rationalistic philosophy which should accomplish what Darwin and Spencer had failed to finish (and this too went to the flames). How in my one poor person I harboured three such clamorously diverse moods, the dominance of which was in part consecutive but in part also synchronistic, or how I contrived to have any intellectual character at all,—I do not know.

But along with these three strands there ran from the beginning a religious impulsion—the strongest of them, I think, though often ought [sic] of sight. This was emphatically dominant in childhood, suffered from scepticism in adolescence, and was mutilated and all but destroyed by rationalism. Its reappearance, I fear, shows signs of that mutilation. But even when most submerged it was there, pushing this way and that for egress and searching for some philosophical justification of its existence. Then, in 1891, I chanced upon Baur's *Das Manichäische Religionssystem,*—how I do not remember. Such mental excitement as that book gave me I had never known before and have never felt since. It was as if the religious sense, like a drowning man, had laid hold of something solid to which it could cling. This was the principle of dualism,—a crude mechanical sort of philosophy as taught by the Manicheans, but through the really magnificent allegory in which their mythology flowered hinting at a deeper and subtler truth.

From that time what I see, looking at my writings objectively, is a series of studies in which, so far as they are literary, classicism is gradually strangling the old romantic remnants, while, so far as the religious interest appears, the newly discovered principle of dualism expresses itself in various affiliations. First it takes the hue of romanticism, seeking a medium in medieval mysticism more or less conflated with the mysticism of the Upanishads, as in *The Great Refusal* (genuine letters, I may say quite privately, though with some fictitious additions at the end and with local alterations by way of disguise). Then it purges itself of medievalism and finds its body in the Hindu contrast of Brahma and Mâyâ, *vidyâ* and *avidyâ,* as expressed in the *Century of Indian Epigrams.* As the sway of Oriental thought wanes, it next evaporates, so to speak, into a kind of thin velleity of absolute faith purified of all myth or dogma or even definite belief, as in the essay on Newman.

Up to this point the religious evolution seems to be strangely lagging behind the literary. But in the end classicism comes to its own in religious philosophy as well as in taste. The result is a transition from India and a sort of thin disembodied Hinduism to Greece, showing itself in attachment to the doctrine of Ideas and phenomena, first in *Platonism,* where the Oriental influence can still be traced, and then more clearly in *The Religion of Plato,* and finally in the Christian Platonism, or Platonic Christianity, of the later volumes. Here *The Catholic Faith* is the τελος.[3]

Although the account given in this letter is fairly comprehensive, it needs to be supplemented from other sources. More's earliest religious training was Presbyterian. During his childhood, he records in "Marginalia," he was generally content in this "Calvinist" faith, and the problems of dualism hardly vexed him. But by his late teens and early twenties he regarded the rigid logic of Calvinism as its greatest weakness, believing that the destruction of any one article of belief would demolish the whole system. From the assumption that God is "the absolute unconditioned Cause of all things," Calvin reasoned to all those logical consequences which theologians had approached for ages without ever really admitting. In this rigid theological form, religion dominated More's childhood; as he grew older, he began to doubt.

Then, one Sunday when he was in his early twenties—1886 seems the likely year, although the date is not certain[4]—he heard a sermon apparently on the subject of universal depravity, and it occasioned his break with Christianity: "With something like a paroxysm of certainty, with bitter actual tears of regret, I cast off once and for all, the faith that had nurtured the better life of my childhood and youth." He admits that this account, given so long after the event, is perhaps colored by later experience and reflection and that he might not have been quite so aware of the theological issues as he later became, he admits also that he was repelled by only a particular form of Christian doctrine rather than the whole. Nevertheless, he turned in fact from the whole of Christianity "and with that for the time being all realization of the noetic life. I left the church that forenoon as one goes out of a spiritual home to wander in the bleak ways of an alien world" ("Marginalia," pp. 23-25). We find him in 1888 declining his mother's invitation to join a Presbyterian Church in St. Louis because he did not believe as a Christian and, so far as he could tell, never would;[5] and he reported in 1889 that Renan's *Vie de Jésus* "almost precisely" summarized his own beliefs.[6]

More's objections to Presbyterianism or Calvinism can be seen more clearly from his essay on Jonathan Edwards (*SE*, XI, 35-65), toward whom he reacted much as he must have reacted to the preacher of that Sunday sermon. Reading Edwards in preparation for his essay, More complained that he had been turned "for the nonce, into a complete atheist."[7] Although he considered Edwards' treatise on the will the greatest philosophical work ever done in America,[8] he believed that, by riddling the Arminian argument for freedom of the will, Edwards had left men only the equally repugnant alternatives of theological determinism or atheism (*SE*, XI, 63). Edwards had one of the clearest perceptions of dualism ever known, but he was led by the spirit of his age and the habit of theologians to personify good and evil as God and the devil. Unlike most men, who seldom think of good and evil as absolutes or who do not consistently identify them with God and the devil, Edwards was "horribly logical and monstrously brave." Accordingly, he is one of the most instructive warnings in history of the evils of mingling an unflinching mythology with a rigid philosophy, for once one grants the legitimacy of accepting a rigid personification of absolute dualism, one has all the explanation needed for the conception of a God who dangles sinners over the pit of hell.[9]

More never lost his belief that the rationalistic formulation of religious experience—though what he would call "rationalistic" would be only rational to others—produced conclusions unacceptable to the human mind. "I would not presume to question the design of Providence," he later wrote, "for God's ways are not as our ways; but to ask me to believe that a just and omnipotent Deity chooses to fashion human beings to the end of dishonour is to quench the only light I have in this dark world and to make a mockery of my moral sense. I should prefer to leave those ultimate causes untouched in their remote obscurity; but if you force me to decide, I would rather waive the omnipotence than the goodness of God."[10] In short, "Man is intellectually impotent and morally responsible"[11]—and that is as neat a summary as he ever made of his conception of man's relationship to God.

There is some suggestion in *Pages from an Oxford Diary* that More's loss of religious faith was at least partly attributable to those contrary influences, romanticism and rationalism, which he mentions to Robert Shafer. When he fell "by a fatal mischance" under the influence of German romanticism, his thoughts of God were supplanted by "a morbid introspection" and his practical worship by an "indulgence in a self-commiserating egotism." As he grew more and more isolated and wretched under this mood, he took solace in the assurance that he was predestined to a great mission and that his despair would lead somehow to his own salvation and to that of mankind. He even began an epic, mentioned in the letter to Shafer, in which he himself figured as the hero, in the guise of the Wandering Jew.

During these years his only God was the image of his own "vague desires, as it were a subtle quintessence of the fermentation of the flesh"; his only peace came "in moments of nervous relaxation when self and the world swam together in a kind of vertiginous dream"; and his only philosophy "was the reaction of a despairing disillusion, a sense of emptiness, out of which the phantasmagoria of life swirls up like a seething mist only to sink back into eternal vacuity." After this romantic indulgence— or perhaps contemporaneously with it, as the letter to Shafer suggests—More turned to rationalism and materialism and conceived the project of a mathematical "New Philosophy" to prove once and for all that man was the product of cosmic chance and probability. What saved him "from moral and emotional paralysis," he believes, was "a deep-seated interest in humanity." He could neither believe that men were machines nor reconcile his own experience of the human will with a mechanism of blind chance and fate.[12] Despite his rejection of Christianity, More was obsessed by an awareness "of a mystery beyond the senses, out of which my dualist philosophy was to spring, those intimations of a whole ghostly world corresponding to something latent in the soul itself" ("Marginalia," 25-26). It was in this state of mind that he came upon Baur and found the clue to explain the mystery.

II *Oriental Dualism*

More saw from the start "the extravagance and materialistic tendencies of the Manichean superstition," and he was taken by Manes' doctrines only because they suggested, in their symbolism of a "cosmic conflict of light and darkness," a solution of the mystery of the mingling of good and evil, for which More so far had found no satisfactory solution in Christianity. Manicheism, in short, acted on him merely "as a powerful stimulus to the imagination" (*SE*, VI, 66)—although there is more than one suggestion in his writings that he never altogether threw off the Manichean conception of a good God struggling against the powers of Darkness. Thirty-five years after his reading of Baur, we find him writing that he views sudden death and physical evil not as providential occurrences, nor as the substance of this life, but as "hateful accidents, or as the working of some no less hideous fatality, breaking through and thwarting the real purpose of the world."[13] And in *Pages from an Oxford Diary*, his last published work, he confesses his belief in a finite God who slowly and with great difficulty imposes His order on the dark Necessity of primordial chaos.[14] These bare hints of an explanation of the causes of evil are two of the very few examples in More of any tendency toward that rationalizing of the bare data of consciousness which he always abhorred.

At any rate, indoctrinated into Oriental philosophy by his study of the Manichees, More turned to the religion and philosophy of India and went east to Harvard in 1892 for the study of Sanskrit and Pali. He was first attracted, he notes, to the Brahmanic theosophy of the Upanishads, but he found that Oriental philosophy of any variety satisfied him to the extent that it demanded no assent to those elements in Christianity which had repelled him. Oriental philosophy was a creed, to use the term loosely, with no omnipotent God, no "apparatus of Platonic Ideas," no heaven or hell, but with an appeal to "what might be called pure spirituality," to something deeper than soul, "to that in us which has no attachment to the phenomenal world or to concrete experience" ("Marginalia," 26).

In 1894 More published a fictional and, we hope, an exaggerated account—done in a mixture of prose and poetry "of a style which will scarcely be popular"[15]—of his embracing of Oriental philosophy. *The Great Refusal* consists of a collection of letters and poems written by a young man of excessively romantic temperament to a woman he calls the Lady Esther. If it is typical of the fiction he might have continued to write, we commend his decision to give himself to critical rather than to creative writing (*SE*, I, 2). As an autobiographical document, *The Great Refusal* points in two directions: it is a farewell to the romantic indulgence of More's earlier life and an acceptance of the detachment of Hindu philosophy. At the beginning of the book the Lady Esther is the hero's symbol of universal beauty, the queen before whom he will lay all the treasures of philosophy

and art. She means to him, he protests, what the Virgin meant to
the medieval mystics: "Here in my own way I have found the
Mother of God" (85-86). Like St. Augustine, he is seeking a
city—not the *Civitas Dei,* but "a *Civitas Amoris,* where the great
Queen rules" (91). The Lady is *"Domina mea"* (93); "You ask
me," he tells her, "if there is nothing better in the world to love
and worship than a woman. There is not" (122). But his disappointments with Western thought take him to Oriental philosophy, from which he learns that beauty is the most dangerous of
illusions, the attraction which more than any other lures men
into satisfaction with their imperfect condition. The true aim of
philosophy, he learns, is isolation and "inattachment" (8); beauty
has no part in securing them. Out of this realization comes the
great refusal—renunciation of the Lady Esther and all she stands
for. More had apparently come to a similar realization.[16]

The culminating section of the sacred writings of the Hindus
is the Upanishads, which are unique among the four main divi-
sions—the Samkita, the Brahmanas, and the Aranyakas being the
other three—in that they require the performance of no action
but merely reveal the truth which emancipates a man from the
vicissitudes of finite existence. The teachings of the Upanishads
never gave rise to a single orthodoxy but produced instead six
"classical" systems of philosophy based on the interpretations of
various commentators and all claiming the infallible authority
of the scriptures. There are also several heterodox systems which
do not claim such authority. More was attracted to the sacred
writings because he saw in them the gropings of many minds
toward the realization that the infinite within and the infinite
without are identical; and he was satisfied by the philosophical
systems, among which there are many similarities, to the extent
that they demand no assent to the literal truth of their allegories.
He was especially attracted to Vedanta, the most influential and
widespread of the classical systems.

The fundamental ideas of the Upanishads are Brahma and
atman. Atman is the name of that element in the self which
underlies the separate acts of our spiritual life—something analogous to what Western thought terms "the soul." Brahma is the
infinite power which creates, sustains, and manifests itself in all
things and into which all things will eventually dissolve. It is
not, however, the equivalent of the Christian conception of God;

for Brahma's power is impersonal and inactive, and its precise nature is incomprehensible to reason.

Equally incomprehensible is the nature of all material and all finite things, including the human soul. Though apparently real, these things are merely illusion—phenomena that exist somewhere between reality and nothing. The Hindu calls them "maya." Since the infinite cannot consist of parts, Brahma and atman are one; and atman, it follows, is aloof from all the turmoils and limitations of personality. It is therefore from within the self that man must seek true knowledge of existence and release, through union with Brahma, from temporal limitations.

Because ultimate reality eludes rational comprehension, Hindu philosophy accepts metaphor, allegory, and mythology as necessary modes of thought, though it regards as illusions such conceptions as that of a personal God. Vedanta, for example, distinguishes between a higher or philosophical knowledge, which proclaims the sole existence of the impersonal Brahma, and a lower or common-sense knowledge which endows Brahma with personality, makes the human soul a vital and independent principle, and provides men with the object of worship their ignorance demands. But however useful that object may be as a center of pious devotion and as a preliminary means of escape from egotism, liberation of the spirit comes through true knowledge alone—not through any false knowledge or through any combination of knowledge and religious performance.[17]

While the influence of these Oriental ideas is widely evident in the *Shelburne Essays* and in other things More was writing at about the same time, it is characteristic of his use of any religious or philosophical system to take from it what suits his purpose. Vedanta proclaims the sole existence of the all-absorbing Brahma; Sankhya, another of the classical systems, holds that two independent essences, nature and spirit, coexist from all eternity. More offhandedly declares that "the two systems are morally one" (*Great Refusal*, 7); and his own Hinduism is either an eclectic derivation from several systems or—what is more likely—a product of his own study of the early writings from which the commentators derived their systems. The Hindu, he says, had "a keen perception of the dual nature of man and the world at large; and this holds true even in the Vedanta, commonly cited as the most radical of monistic systems."[18] In "The Forest Philosophy of India" (*SE*, VI, 1-42), he argues his own dualist reading of the sacred writings against the non-dualist interpretations of both ancient sage and modern scholar. Certainly More was never in the strict sense a believer: he went to Vedanta only "for strength and consolation" and to fortify his isolated life "with the virtue and dignity of experience" (*Century*, 18-19). Besides, it was not long before he had given up Vedanta for Platonism.

III *From Hinduism to Platonism*

It is impossible to assign a precise chronology to More's progress from Hinduism to Platonism, but in addition to the autobiographical writings and passages we have already seen there are a number of essays that reflect his departure from the position attained by the hero of *The Great Refusal*—particularly "Delphi and Greek Literature" (1898), "Nemesis, or the Divine Envy" (1899), and "Socrates" (1909).[19] "Delphi and Greek Literature" (*SE*, II, 188-218) and "Nemesis, or the Divine Envy" (*SE*, II, 219-53), which followed *The Great Refusal* by four and five years, respectively, evince the beginnings of the change. The genius of the Greeks, More says, is contained in their discovery of the value of temperance and self-restraint. "Nothing too much" was their maxim for the regulation of outer conduct and "Know thyself" for that of inner. The first governed morality and art, the second was the beginning and end of philosophy; through the two, the Greeks progressed to Epicurean tranquillity and Stoic apathy. The next step would have been the "inattachment" of the Hindu. The Hindu, seeing himself in an illusory world with no discoverable relationship to his deepest religious needs, withdrew from the world as much as possible, performed the duties of his station without interest in the result, and took to contemplation as a means of renunciation and peace. The Greek, on the contrary, saw nature as complementary to himself, contemplated it with joy, and gave himself actively to worldly affairs. The Hindu thus reached a stage of selflessness and religious development beyond the achievement of the Greek, who was often selfish and short-sighted; but the Greek ideal is more completely and naturally human. In brief, More asserts in these essays the intellectual and moral, though not the religious, superiority of the Greek because his moderation and humanism constitutes a more satisfactory response to the world of total experience than does the other-worldliness of the Hindu.

In "Socrates" (*SE*, VI, 242-69) More's acceptance of the Greek ideal is wholehearted and explicit, for he acknowledges Socrates, the embodiment of that ideal, as his personal guide in both religion and philosophy. The essay comes toward the end of a volume subtitled *Studies of Religious Dualism,* in which More examines several of the great religious figures of history in the hope of discovering some religious standard which outlasts the rise and fall of successive creeds. The Hindu sages, he finds, will hardly do, for they are too shadowy in themselves to serve as effective examples and their doctrine is too remote and austere for the Western world. Christ is equally unsatisfactory, both because He "is involved completely in the historic error of Christianity" and because of some inherent defect in His "feminine gospel of love for God and man. . . . I can only speak of what I know," More concludes, "and for me, as one deceptive hope after another has fallen away, I go back to the life of Socrates and the reasoning of Plato and am never deceived. I am assured that they were seeking what I seek, and that they attained what hardly and with their borrowed strength I may at last attain" (246-47). "Plato" (*SE*, VI, 321-46), the concluding essay of the volume, deals with the man who developed the religious insights of his master into a systematic philosophy; in it More presents his own conception of the true religious instinct —the compromise, that is, with which he was then content, between his religious inclinations and his antipathy to fixed creed.

The religious instinct in its essential purity, he writes, lies "in the bare consciousness of a dual tendency in human nature" (321). We are drawn in one direction toward unity and the absorption of our separate desires in the sense of our own completeness, and the recognition of this integrity distracts us from the contrary awareness of our individuality and incompleteness. This centripetal tendency we call the spiritual ideal as opposed to the material; its goal is a state of changelessness and participation in the infinite. But we are drawn simultaneously to the world of variety and change and desire, which culminates in death. These opposing tendencies are equally real and impressive; even those who deny one and accept the other see on occasion the insufficiency of their choice. One of the great advantages of Platonism is that it gives equal recognition to the duality of experience. It was conceived among a people who had never been dominated by either a priesthood or a divine revelation and for whom theology was, consequently, a product of human fancy. For this reason the religion of Plato, despite his occasional divagations into myth-making and metaphysical reasoning, "is at heart thoroughly human" (325); its kernel is the incontrovertible fact of dualism.

Another figure in whom More discovered an almost perfect understanding of dualism was Emerson, whom he studied seriously at about the time he was formulating his own dualism and his belief in the possibility of a "pure" religion uncontaminated by dogma or ritual. Plato, he admitted, had "perhaps alone of philosophers" reconciled the Greek notion of the infinite with the Oriental notion of impersonality; but Emerson made this Platonic discovery "the kernel of his doctrine" (*SE*, VIII, 26). More concluded in 1894, the year of *The Great Refusal* and not long after his reading of Baur, that anyone who understood the meaning of dualism as Emerson propounded it in "Fate" had no need to study Sanskrit for the wisdom of the east.[20] Much of Emerson's appeal for More lay in his belief that Emerson made the same promises of liberation as Buddha and Christ but without imposing a discipline or doctrine upon his followers and that, unlike the Hindu, he never brooded over the insufficiency of earthly life or sought to escape it through philosophical dogmatism or asceticism. His deep confidence in the power of the soul made him instead an optimist (*SE*, I, 76-81). This same optimism, however, led to Emerson's one great failing: he was deficient in moral insight. Emerson's blithe dismissal of the reality of evil made his dualism finally "a vanishing dualism" (*SE*, XI, 87), and left him an unsatisfactory guide for anyone who required that religion and philosophy deal with all the facts of experience (*SE*, XI, 88-89).

It would be impossible to trace all the influences that led More through the development I have just sketched. Some of them we have noted, and More himself credited Irving Babbitt with being the most important formative influence on his mind after their meeting in 1892.[21] But More's progress from Calvinism to Platonism through romanticism, rationalism, and Oriental theosophy reflects also the strengthening of certain temperamental traits which are evident in him from his childhood: a strong affection for human beings, a need for imaginative and emotional satisfaction, and a strong ethical bent. It was "a deep-seated interest in humanity" (*Oxford Diary,* sec. V) which led him to give up the rationalist materialism of his youth; and, just as he could not then believe that men were machines, so he could not later accept that debasement of mankind to which Oriental philosophy inevitably led. The Hindu belief in the illusoriness of the phenomenal and personal world came to seem just as inhuman to More as philosophical mechanism, or theological determinism for that matter, had earlier seemed. He might continue for some years to speak of "the illusory nature of the world" and "of a reality of which this life is only the shadow,"[22] but these expressions took on more conventional Christian implications. "In one sense," he would write in *Pages from an Oxford Diary,* "the world to any man of insight appears illusory. . . . But illusion in the sense that all this manifold display of life, the constant efflorescense of beauty, the noble aspirations and warm affections of the living human heart, are meaningless riddles, phantom bubbles out of vacuity, insubstantial forms and inconsequential events, with no purpose behind them, with no relation to a permanent world of peace and justice and truth, with no characters of love written upon them by a designing mind—illusion in that sense I cannot accept" (sec. XV).

What I have referred to as More's need for imaginative and emotional satisfaction is perhaps merely the positive aspect of the anti-rationalism we have seen in his views on religion and will later see in his views on science. It is worth noting that of the two opposing tendencies he experienced in himself in his youth, materialistic rationalism and romantic emotionalism, he was much more successful in throwing off the former. He was always temperamentally something of a romantic. When he began his Oriental studies at Harvard he was attracted to Sanskrit and Vedanta because of the romantic richness he found in them (*NSE,* III, 33); all his life he responded to sentiment, emotion, and sensuous appeal. We should not be confused, therefore, by the anti-romantic tenor of the *Shelburne Essays.* More himself came to attribute "the note of personal bitterness" in his attacks on romantic writers and particularly on Wordsworth (as in *SE,* VII, 27-43) to his deliberate attempt to divorce himself from romantic influences and to refashion his taste on the classics.[23] And to come back to his early religious development, he came to prefer Platonism to Hinduism because of the imaginative attraction of the historical Socrates and because Hindu asceticism, as he makes clear in "Delphi and Greek Literature," gave little encouragement to the practice of art, the cultivation of beauty.

Nor, finally, was Hindu asceticism as productive in the realm of conduct as the Greek ideal of moderation; it was a harsh extreme without incentive for social or civilized life. More's concern with the world of conduct causes him, despite his rejection of Calvinist doctrine, to admire "that sturdiness and uprightness of character, which was one of the great, the very great, compensations of Puritanism" (*SE*, XI, 20); we will presently see the importance he attaches to the well-being of society.

More significant than the changes in his religious and philosophical beliefs is the continuity running through them, for his studies of Oriental and Western religion and philosophy, whatever else they might be, are attempts to find confirmation of the revelations of his own consciousness in the wider experience of mankind. All through the period of the *Shelburne Essays* and well into the 1920's, although again no precise dating is possible, he was engaged in a search for a "creedless faith" or "pure spirituality." He found his first clue to such a quality in Manicheism, and he went from there to the philosophies of India, and chiefly to Vedanta, where he found dualism in a more acceptable formulation. But finding these philosophies also emotionally and imaginatively unsatisfactory, he turned to the person of Socrates and the philosophy of Plato, where, as he thought, he had finally found true religion. The essential continuity of this development is indicated in his manner of elaborating Vedanta and Platonism alike in the same idiom.[24] When he published *Platonism* in 1917, he anticipated the charge that he was forcing Plato into the pattern of his Vedantic dualism, as he had outlined it in 1913 in the essay "Definitions of Dualism" (*SE*, VIII, 247-302). Those definitions, he said, were themselves a result of his study of Plato.[25] Yet he later admitted that "the Oriental influence can still be traced" in *Platonism*,[26] which "presents almost completely the same point of view as the sixth volume of *Shelburne Essays*."[27]

IV *"Definitions of Dualism"*

"Definitions of Dualism" is not an argument, but a compilation of definitions of the fundamentals of More's dualism and of their various implications in thought and conduct. It is his most explicit and systematic presentation of the standards he had been using in his writings down to the date of its appearance; he would continue to use these standards for some time to come. Its aphoristic quality makes it somewhat difficult to summarize, but because of its importance for any discussion of More's work, I give a brief and partial summary of it.

There is an opposition within the human consciousness, says More, between two irreconcilable forces—an incessant flux of desires and impressions and an inner check which opposes them. These forces are the fundamental elements of consciousness; we can know nothing more about them than the mere fact that they exist. The sum of phenomena, including the human body, is nature; what remains in the self, after nature is distinguished, is the soul. Some part of the soul, however—the temperament— belongs to the flux, and the soul has no immortal existence apart from the body. The dualism of body and soul is an external or secondary dualism only, the fundamental dualism being the one we have already described—the opposition of inner check and outward desire within the consciousness itself. When nature appears to be under the control of some force analogous to the inner check, we call it beautiful. We are inspired by natural beauty because it suggests the indwelling of some supernal force; we are consoled by it because it symbolizes the possible happiness of the soul. Such consolation, however, is an illusion; the only sure consolation is our knowledge that something within us stands apart from the flux.

Art is the attempt to establish the experience of the individual in tradition, and the arts may be arranged in an ascending scale of dignity according as the sense to which each is primarily directed has less of the flux and more of stability in its activity: odor, sound, color and line, form. Literature, the artistic use of language, is less intense and precise in its effects than the more sensuous arts, but it is broader, more profound, and more es- sentially a function of life. Within any given art, individual works tend to perfection insofar as the artist's imagination is con- trolled by the inner check. Talent is a man's ability to express his experience; genius is the degree to which the consciousness of dualism enters into that expression. Tradition is the collective experience of society, and the chief function of education is to transfer the wealth of a selective tradition from society to the individual.

Reason is the faculty by which we understand and meet the flux, but being itself a part of the flux, it tends to deny and usurp the power of the inner check. When it denies the duality of consciousness and seeks to explain the whole of reality by only one of the halves, it falls into one or another of various and often overlapping errors to which More gives the generic designation of metaphysics. Metaphysics thus takes two general forms, depending on whether it bases itself on our sense of unity or of diversity; but within these two general forms are many short-lived varieties and a number of persistent ones. Rationalism is the attempt to raise reason to an independent and predominant place in the soul and to deny the reality of all that lies beyond the comprehension of reason. Naturalism is the assumption of nature and the soul under the same law of nature. Modern pragmatism is one variety of naturalism, but any rationalism is a naturalism simply because the reason is entirely a creature of nature. Romanticism is a radical confusion of the unlimited desires with the inner check, and it most often shows itself as a restless intensification of personal emotion. As romanticism turns away from reason it is opposed to rationalism, but because it confounds the true infinite with the finite, it is, along with rationalism, simply another variety of naturalism. In a scientific age such as ours, metaphysics takes a scientific form. In the strict sense, science is the systematic accumulation of knowledge; more broadly, it is the attempt to express the observations of the senses in the abstract conceptions of reason. But when it goes beyond positive observation and scientific hypothesis in order to explain reality by some universal law, it passes into metaphysical reasoning.

The safeguard against all such errors is self-knowledge, which we call "insight" when it works in a positive manner under the direction of a consciousness of dualism, and "skepticism" when it prohibits the supplanting of dualism by the abstractions of the reason. Insight and skepticism, however, are not to be confused with doubt, for doubt is only mental lethargy and another source of error. Self-knowledge grows with the exercise of the inner check and results in truth in the intellectual sphere and in morality in the practical. The life of truth is philosophy, and the function of reason in philosophy is to discern the workings of the inner check in the field of the flux. In this capacity, reason is often called intuition.

Character is the control of the impulses by the inner check, and the most useful summary of moral experience is that virtue is the mean between extremes of action. Since men in general are lacking in character, the will to refrain must be supplemented by such external restraints as public opinion, fear of punishment, education, and mythology. Justice, the chief of the civic virtues, produces the same balance in society as character produces in the individual. The theory that justice can be produced by instinctive sympathy alone rests on the assumption that men will act under their natural inclinations in such a way as to effect the happiness and the good of others. Such an assumption is fallacious, for it ignores the fact that personality belongs to the flux and thus naturally tends to variety and difference. Humanitarianism is the social application of this theory.

Government is the political organization of external checks, and the aim of government should be to establish liberty. Primarily an inner condition which results when the impulses and passions are controlled by the inner check, liberty becomes an outer condition when society is so organized as to bring the mass of men, who have no character, under the influence of those who have. The idea of absolute democracy is based upon the assumption that once men are freed of external restraints, they can be truly free—that is, once again, that the human personality is naturally disposed toward order. Belief in absolute democracy is thus another denial of dualism, and it tends naturally toward socialism or anarchy and ultimately toward tyranny or chaos. In the actual condition of the world, that society is freest in which custom and law impose the least restraint upon men of character and the greatest restraint upon the rest.

On the level of true knowledge, our profoundest achievements are insight and skepticism, but it is possible to pass from knowledge to religion; and in mysticism, which is the goal of all true religion and philosophy, we can achieve the cessation of desire and the liberation of consciousness. There are occasional moments in human experience when men's consciousness of the inner check is so strong as to sever temporarily the continuity of their impulsive lives. These moments are an assurance of the possibility of lasting peace. The assurance itself is faith, and its counterpart is disillusion with the world, just as the counterpart of insight is skepticism. Beneath the apparent order of the world, we see the chaos of the flux; we know that life is mere appearance and ourselves mere illusion. The hope of immortality is the yearning for a life freed from the flux, an anticipation of the eternal liberation of the spirit.

Faith and disillusion are therefore the positive and negative sides of spirituality, and the life of spirituality is religion. Mythology is the peopling of the unknown with anthropomorphic beings; it can be either a spontaneous and unreasoned product of the imagination or a deliberate product of reason. Rational mythologies closely resemble the metaphysical hypotheses of science, insofar as they admit only what is acceptable to reason; their insufficiency is that they leave no room for the reality of evil. They do not, like faith, surmount it; they merely deny it. Belief, not to be confused with faith, is the acceptance of the reality of mythology and of mythological figures. The various Christian mysteries are symbolic renderings of the truths of dualism, although Christian mythology opposes a perfectly righteous deity to the depraved human soul. Theology is the attempt to impose the abstractions of metaphysics on the personal dualism of spontaneous mythology, but it invariably ends either by destroying mythology or by giving way to superstition. When mythology ends, the alternatives are rationalism or insight. Skepticism acts in religion by simultaneously withholding belief in mythology and accepting the mystery from which it springs.

It is easy to object to "Definitions of Dualism." In its psychology or epistemology, if I may use a term whose applicability More would deny, there is an arbitrary vagueness—a refusal, however justified by the definitions themselves, to admit any rational analysis of fundamental principles and conceptions. This refusal is a manifestation of that anti-rationalism I have already noted in More's temperament; it shows itself here not only in his denial of the absolute supremacy of reason, but also in his insistence that certain questions are simply not open to reason at all. At the same time, the schematization of artistic forms, as of mental faculties too (*SE,* VIII, 251-57), which this summary has not included, seems unsophisticated and wooden—an imposition of fine-spun and *a priori* categories. But the distrust of reason, in both secular and sacred affairs, is the most apparent mark of the essay.

"It is odd, but true," he writes elsewhere, "that reasonableness and rationalism have never been able to dwell together peacefully,"[28] and we see perfectly that he is saying nothing which is not supported by history. Yet his reaction to the extravagances of reason produces at times an extravagance of its own which is little less than shocking in so knowledgeable a man. "Pretty much all the truth of Freudianism," he writes, "can be found in the Platonic and Stoic theory of dreams" (*NSE*, I, 22). Metaphysics, he writes, attempts to "hold the universe in a syllogism, denying thereby all our concrete experience, all our sense of multiplicity and change, all our knowledge of evil, denying life for an abstract unity of the reason" (*SE*, VII, 200). Yet Thomism—to cite one system of thought in which metaphysics has a place—denies neither concrete experience nor multiplicity and change, and Catholic theology—certainly metaphysical—speaks of the mystery of evil. The remark in "Definitions of Dualism" that Christianity opposes a righteous deity to the depraved human soul (*SE*, VIII, 296) indicates that More still has Calvinism in mind when he speaks of Christianity. Yet, even after he had become more familiar with other systems of Christian doctrine, he continued in his suspicion of metaphysical theology—and of Roman Catholicism in particular.[29] Simply stated, his belief is that reason cannot encompass experience. Most of us agree that it cannot, but we think it can encompass a good bit more of experience than More thinks it can. More has a great relish for Samuel Johnson's retort to the determinism of Jonathan Edwards: "All theory is against the freedom of the will, all experience for it" (*SE*, XI, 63). Yet it is difficult to see how the attempt to exploit the full potential of reason, whatever the dangers of rationalism, is any less valid than More's limitation of reason, or any less truly human.

Finally, "Definitions of Dualism" may seem suspiciously simple. But the very conception of the essay requires simplicity since the detailed arguing of so many "definitions" would take a book of considerable size. And More's other writings, of course, are that book.

Whatever its faults, "Definitions of Dualism" defines the standards of the *Shelburne Essays*. More's views changed somewhat in later years, but changed very little, if at all, in any fundamental way. He gave up the Vedantic conceptions still evident in this essay, made certain changes in his terminology and emphasis, and even became reconciled to theological dogma —though only to the barest minimum of dogma and in his own formulation of it. But he never renounced the philosophical dualism he defines here or any of its major implications for philosophy, morality, society, or literature.

A passage in "The Quest of a Century" shows how important the conception is in his criticism of individuals, societies, and traditions: "It is possible, I believe, to view the ceaseless intellectual fluctuations of mankind backward and forward as the varying fortunes of the contest between these two hostile members of our being,—between the deep-lying principle that impels us to seek rest and the principle that drags us back into the region of change and motion and forever forbids us to acquiesce in what is found. And I believe further that the moral disposition of a nation or of an individual may be best characterised by the predominance of the one or the other of these two elements" (*SE*, III, 245).

CHAPTER 2

Criticism

I *Organization of the* Shelburne Essays

THE *Shelburne Essays* is a series of eleven volumes of collected essays which More published from 1904 to 1921. Although some of the volumes are unified in theme or subject—the sixth, *Studies of Religious Dualism;* the eighth, on romanticism; the ninth, on politics and society; and the tenth, on the tradition of wit in English literature—very few of the essays in these volumes appeared in them originally, and all of the volumes have a somewhat arbitrary appearance, with the possible exception of the sixth. While nine of the eleven essays in *With the Wits: Shelburne Essays, Tenth Series* treat English writers of the Restoration and the eighteenth century, there is also one on Beaumont and Fletcher and another on Wilde and his circle. These, the first and last essays in the book, describe the origins and the culmination of the tradition of wit as More defines it, but the volume nevertheless looks like a study of the Restoration and the eighteenth century with a couple of loosely related pieces attached; at the same time there is no essay on Samuel Johnson. In his Preface, More acknowledges the looseness of his design. Most of the other volumes have even less unity, either of time or of subject matter; and some of the topics or figures treated in them are likely to strike the contemporary reader as insignificant or bizarre. More once admitted that his work gave him "the impression of a mind groping about and not knowing whither it is bound. The field is too wide and the effect scattered. I seem not to be one intelligence but an unassimilated bundle of impulses and curiosities."[1]

The unfortunate arrangement is easily explained. Most of the essays of which the volumes are composed are pieces which he published separately in a number of places between 1898 and 1921. Some are the products of his literary journalism; some were originally lectures; some, expressions of his personal interests. Both Irving Babbitt and William Roscoe Thayer advised him that certain of his works—*Studies of Religious Dualism* specifically—would be more impressive if published independently of the series; but More objected, probably with the example of Sainte-Beuve in mind, that his reputation would in the long run depend largely on the "very bulk and massiveness" of his output.[2] The disorder of the *Shelburne Essays*, therefore, is immediately chargeable to his decision to publish a continuing series and, beyond that, to his energy, the range of his mind, and his longevity.

It would be shortsighted, however, to regard the *Shelburne Essays* merely as an undirected collection of random essays. There is little doubt that if they were rearranged and properly indexed—the only indexing consists of lists in the seventh, tenth, and eleventh volumes of titles and principal subjects—they would constitute a more useful and more coherent work. But even in their present arrangement they have a range and depth which no mere rearrangement would increase. They treat English literature of all periods except the Middle Ages, with particular emphasis on British literature of the seventeenth, eighteenth, and nineteenth centuries and on the literature of New England; Greek and Oriental literature, including translations from Greek and Sanskrit; religion and philosophy, including Hindu, Greek, Christian, and modern; education, political and social philosophy, and the philosophical implications of science. A list of the authors treated is particularly impressive. Among the better known figures are Arnold, St. Augustine, Berkeley, Blake, Browning, Bunyan, Byron, Carlyle, Dickens, Jonathan Edwards, Emerson, Franklin, Hawthorne, Huxley, William James, Keats, Lamb, Milton, Newman, Nietzsche, Pascal, Plato, Poe, Pope, Rousseau, Sainte-Beuve, Scott, Shakespeare, Shelley, Socrates, Sterne, Swift, Tennyson, Thoreau, Tolstoy, Whitman, Wordsworth, and Yeats. The names of the lesser figures may not much increase the luster of the list, but they show something further of More's range and interests: Thomas Bailey Aldrich, Beaumont and Fletcher, Aphra Behn, Sir Thomas Browne, Fanny Burney, Samuel Butler, Lord Chesterfield, Cowper, Crabbe, Samuel Crisp, G. Lowes Dickinson, Disraeli, and so on through the alphabet. There is not an essay in the lot which is not competent and, within the limits of More's critical aims, balanced and thorough.

His purpose, he once said, was to compose "a kind of history of human thought and ideals of life," chiefly in England but with excursions into other countries.[3] Another purpose is implicit in the excerpt he took from James Russell Lowell for the epigraph to *Shelburne Essays, First Series*: "Before we have an American literature, we must have an American criticism." How long More consciously followed either purpose is a question. The word "history" suggests a systematic presentation, but "a kind of" is a liberating if vague qualification, and an American literature might be stimulated by any good criticism, whether systematically marshaled or not. The historical intent is reflected in the volumes which are thematically unified as well as in individual essays scattered throughout the series. Like other students of intellectual history, More believed that human society could profitably be studied in terms of certain important issues which recur and interact throughout history. Natural and moral law, faith and reason, and the opposition of liberal and conservative tendencies within the individual and society are some of the larger issues that interest him; deism, humanitarianism, historical romanticism, and Darwinian evolution are some of the smaller. But since *Shelburne Essays* is primarily a collection of independent essays, each relatively brief, limited in scope, and focusing for the most part on individual figures for whom the historical discussions are only part of a necessary background, More's historiography, if we may call it that, is piecemeal and repetitious, though consistent with itself and comprehensive when taken as a whole.

For example, in "Victorian Literature" (*SE*, VII, 245-69) he contends that the chief literary accomplishment of the Victorian age was the unifying of science and poetry, which are usually thought of as essentially opposed. The poetic sources of the nineteenth century, he says, go back to Wordsworth, for though Wordsworth's return to nature was a logical consequence of Rousseau's philosophy and, beyond that, of the philosophy of English deism, there is a profound distinction between Wordsworth and the philosophers of the preceding century. When the deists of the eighteenth century thought of man as a purely natural being, they dismissed from consideration all those elements in man which we associate with the supernatural. The natural man of their natural world is unperturbed by cravings which cannot be satisfied from within nature. There is thus no confusion among them of the natural and the supernatural; the latter is simply excluded from the former. But when Wordsworth turned to nature he did so with all the fervor which earlier ages had reserved for supernatural religion, thereby introducing the great pathetic fallacy which has bewildered poets ever since.

Thus it came about during the nineteenth century that as science tried to reduce the flux of the natural order to scientific law, poetry gave emotional expression to the same flux. All through Victorian literature we find clear evidence of the effects of the philosophy of change on the substance and form of English verse. William Morris contemplated a swiftly moving phantasmagoria of forms, colors, and melodies, with the fear that should they once pause in their movement they would disappear. Although Swinburne's universe was hardly different, with him the uninterrupted fluxation dissolved the solid earth into endless impressions of wind and water. Browning joyed in the tumult and conflict of life because he accepted them in the assurance that things right themselves of their natural tendencies. In America, Walt Whitman gazed on "a strange motley procession of shifting forms, . . . calling upon no passing appearance to stay for an instant and deliver its meaning" (*SE,* VII, 259). The work of Malthus and Arnold, of Newman and Spencer is imbued with the same spirit of change, whose results we see wherever we look: Darwinism in science, impressionism in the arts, pragmatism in philosophy, laissez faire and Marxism in economics, and the elective system and scientific studies in education in place of the old emphasis on classics and humanities which derived from the conviction that human experience is essentially unchanging "and has once for all been expressed" (256).

But logically, if not by its actual place in the volume in which it appears, "Victorian Literature" is the nucleus of a number of other essays. The ideas expressed in it are developed with greater or lesser completeness in separate essays on most of the figures named in it and on other figures as well—on Wordsworth, Morris, Swinburne, Browning, Whitman, Tennyson, Newman, and Huxley. Still other figures, a good deal more remote from Darwinian science or literary romanticism, are nonetheless connected with the historical process described in "Victorian Literature." Even Bishop Berkeley is involved, for in dissolving the outer world into personality, in depriving phenomena of material reality, he did more than anyone else of his day to destroy the distinction between man and thing (*SE,* X, 220-21).

Thus while the *Shelburne Essays* are in a sense a history of human thought and ideals, the reader who wants More's comprehensive opinion on any extended historical development is not likely to find it in one place. For a history of romanticism in England, the reader would have to supplement *The Drift of Romanticism* with the essays on Blake, Byron, Keats, Scott, Shelley, Swinburne, and others—all to be found elsewhere in the series. In the same way, there is a coherent history of American literature in the *Shelburne Essays,* but until recently the reader has had to dig it out for himself.[4] It is best to admit at the start that the *Shelburne Essays* are a miscellany and to look elsewhere for whatever unity we expect. The essays have not the unity of systematic arrangement, but they are harmonized by a consistent philosophical or moral purpose. More's theory of criticism will serve to introduce that purpose.

II *Criticism*

There was a time when More thought that he would do his best work "in the drama—comedy and tragedy."[5] His first book was a collection of verses, sentimental and conventional; two other early books were novels, more interesting for thematic than fictional content.[6] When, however, during his retreat at Shelburne, New Hampshire—hence the name *Shelburne Essays*—he decided to make criticism his major effort (*SE,* I, 2), he did not think that he was choosing the less worthy pursuit. To his mind, the critic was the equal of the "creative" writer—not, as in the usual view, his inferior: ". . . The best and most durable acts of mankind are the ideals and emotions that go to make up its books, and to describe and judge the literature of a country, to pass under review a thousand systems and reveries, to point out the meaning of each, and so write the annals of the human spirit, to pluck out the heart of each man's mystery and set it before the mind's eye quivering with life,—if this be not a labour of immense creative energy the word has no sense to my ears" (*SE,* III, 76-77).

Criticism, More admits, depends on creative literature insofar as what is judged must precede the judgment; yet the critic is no mere recorder or arbiter of ideas; he is an active, creative force. The best statement of this view is the essay "Criticism" (*SE,* VII, 213-44), in which More writes that while the single work of literature is the product of the dramatist, the novelist, and the poet, literature in its broadest sense is equally the product of the critic. The literature of a people is the expression of its accumulated experience—a racial equivalent of the individual memory, through which the inheritance of an immeasurable past is transmuted into something both greater and less than the actual events out of which it has sprung: less, through having lost the intensity of the vital moment; greater, through being absorbed into a continuing and significant tradition. In the formation of this race memory, the critic plays the most important part: the critic absorbs the past into the present, links the isolated moments into a unified experience, judges and selects or discards.

Quite obviously, the critic as More speaks of him here is not merely the literary critic, just as literature in this context is not *belles lettres* only. More is aware of the pretentions of his claim. "All scholars," he says, "whether they deal with history or sociology or philosophy or language or, in the narrower sense of the word, literature, are servants of the critical spirit, insofar as they transmit and interpret and mould the sum of experience from man to man and from generation to generation" (244). If by this theory literary critics lose their uniqueness, they are compensated for the loss by being joined to "one of the great families of human intelligence . . . : discriminators between the false and the true, the deformed and the normal; preachers of harmony and proportion and order; prophets of the religion of taste" (218). If they deal with literature, they do so only because they find it the best reflection of life and because they hope to make it a criticism of life. Though critics generally suffer by comparison with the more creative figures of history, "their very lack of warping originality" becomes their justification, for they "stand with the great conservative forces of human nature, having their fame certified by the things that endure amid all the betrayals of time and fashion" (220).

While "Criticism" is primarily concerned with Matthew Arnold, it is More's own apology also, and it helps explain some of the peculiarities of the *Shelburne Essays*. The romanticism referred to in *The Drift of Romanticism,* for example, is not only literary romanticism, but a much broader tendency which runs through Western culture from the beginnings of the Christian era. It is "that expansive conceit of the emotions which goes with the illusion of beholding the infinite within the stream of nature itself instead of apart from the stream" (*SE*, VIII, xiii). In *The Drift of Romanticism*, although he confines himself to the nineteenth century, More studies it not only in such literary figures as William Beckford, Pater, and Fiona Macleod, but in Newman, Huxley, and Nietzsche, and through them in the Oxford Movement, evolutionary science, and modern politics at large. Aware of the objections likely to be raised against such a generalized and partial treatment of writers whose claims are so largely unique, More explains that though the highest type of criticism would, while relating writers to their philosophical and historical backgrounds, also judge them on their individual accomplishments, the critic is justified on occasion in practicing a partial or lower type of criticism. More chooses to practice that lower type because he feels compelled to resist the dangerous tendencies of romanticism. As he puts it elsewhere, it is necessary to be arbitrary in order to deal effectively with ideas (*SE*, VII, 245).

The same ideological concern leads him to distinguish between two classes of poets, "the essential" and "the contingent." These are not the same as major and minor. Both Keats and Wordsworth are major poets, but Keats alone is an essential one. Keats's poetry would be the same for us if we had never heard its author's name; we judge it for its intrinsic value. Wordsworth is a contingent poet, some of the best of whose verse takes on value and significance from what we know of his personality and philosophy (*SE*, IV, 21-22). Most of More's criticism is concerned with contingent poets; at least he treats most poets as if he regards them as contingent.

III *Dualism as Critical Standard*

The selection of a tradition requires a principle of selection, and More's principle, in literature as in religion and philosophy, is dualism. We are not surprised to find, therefore, that the literary criticism of the *Shelburne Essays* shows the influence of his Oriental studies. Especially in the earlier volumes do his judgments and analyses make use of such conceptions as maya and karma, the higher and the lower self, self-knowledge, insight, and inattachment. Not all of these terms or the concepts to which they apply are exclusively Hindu, but several of them are; and in the early *Shelburne Essays* More often uses those which are not Hindu in the same context with those which are and as extensions of them. In "Arthur Symons: the Two Illusions" (*SE*, I, 122-46) we are told that the essence of art lies in a combination of illusion and disillusion. By his skill at illusion the poet endows the products of his imagination with such vividness and appeal as to make them appear the truest reality; but if he is a true artist, he must somehow also dispel the enchantment and show us the insubstantiality of what we see. It is impossible to consider the illusion of art "without recurring to the Hindu doctrine of Mâyâ, who is supposed to be the creative force of all this wonderful web of appearances that enwrap the spirit in their mesh and charm the spirit's attention by their mystery of beauty and seeming benevolence" (124). "The Spirit of Carlyle" (*SE*, I, 85-102) praises Carlyle for having "that sense of illusion which we call Oriental and which is really the basis of Hindu religion" (87) and for his instinctive appreciation of the law of karma, "the unvarying law of everlasting cause and effect: what a man sowed that should be inevitably reap" (91).

"Kipling and FitzGerald" (*SE*, II, 104-25) condemns those writers because, although their experience in the Orient should have taught them better, they have failed in the highest obligations of their art. FitzGerald sees the transient nature of the world but nothing permanent beyond it; Kipling never goes beyond his portrayal of the restless activity of the Anglo-Saxon to the deeper energy of the will to refrain. In contrast to the judgment of Kipling and FitzGerald, and as a final example, the surest sign of Hawthorne's greatness—of the profundity and universality of his art—is that he shares with the ancient sages of India a fearsome appreciation of the isolation of the human soul (*SE*, I, 48-49); even Hester Prynne, living out her solitary penance in seventeenth-century Boston, is unconsciously following the Hindu doctrine of inattachment as it is described in the *Bhagavad Gita* (*SE*, I, 36).

As the *Shelburne Essays* progress, the Vedantic terminology tends to disappear, but there is no essential change in More's standards. The essay "Henry Adams" (*SE*, XI, 117-40) is a good deal less obviously Vedantic than the earlier pieces on Carlyle, Symons, Kipling, and FitzGerald, but it is merely an application of definition LXXIV of "Definitions of Dualism" (*SE*, VIII, 291-92). Adams' tragedy is that his personal experience and his formal studies destroyed his belief in the religion and philosophy of his ancestors and that, having no true faith to supplant the one he had lost, he turned to skepticism and doubt. He saw the illusion of worldly existence, but his disillusion was not a true one since it did not show him the true infinite that underlies the flux.

As late as 1936 More held to the conception of poetic illusion he had used in the essay on Symons thirty-four years before, although again there is no longer a suggestion of Oriental terminology. In *The Study of English Literature* he distinguished several types of poetic illusion, of which the highest consists in making the physical world into a symbol of the spiritual and in showing the paradoxical unreality of the finite.[7] But dualism figures prominently not only in More's unconnected essays on individual writers; in the thematically unified volumes of the *Shelburne Essays,* it provides the unifying element. Though *Studies of Religious Dualism* is the most obvious example, the statement is just as true of *The Drift of Romanticism* or *With the Wits.* In *The Drift of Romanticism,* after giving his introductory definition of romanticism, More says: "The question raised finally is thus one of dualism: Is there, or is there not, some element of man's being superior to instinct and reason, some power that acts as a stay upon the flowing impulses of nature, without whose authoritative check reason herself must in the end be swept away in the dissolution of the everlasting flux?" (*SE*, VIII, xiii). In one way or another he applies this question to all the writers he considers in the book.

Besides furnishing More with a thematic or philosophical standard, dualism also helps him in his formal analyses because it is involved in the very nature of poetry. "If any one thing may be called certain in criticism," he writes, "it is that the quintessence of poetical emotion, the very kernel of the bitter-sweet passion of life and the world, arises from the simultaneous perception in man's destiny of the ever-fleeting and of that which is *contrayr to mutabilitie*" (*SE*, VII, 263-64). On this conception, and others derived from it, he works out a rudimentary theory of literary genres.

In "The Scotch Novels and Scotch History" (*SE*, III, 82-99) he begins a discussion of the difference between poetry and prose by calling attention to "some principle of isolation and exclusion" (83-84) which separates us from one another and thwarts the fullest development of our human potential. This is the same limitation which Hawthorne and the ancient Hindus saw as the isolation of the human soul; it is rooted in the dualism of human nature, which is drawn simultaneously toward the sense of its own sufficiency and independence and toward immersion in the flux of outward experience. The function of literature, as of the other arts, is to interpret this thwarting and isolation "and to bestow on us the illusion of unconfined liberty" (84); the different genres perform the function in different ways.

Epic and dramatic poetry achieve this end through concentration and intensity; they give us in the character of the hero not so much the separate man as the typical man, through whom, because he speaks and acts with the greatest passion and freedom, we seem to escape from the limitations of our private selves. The effect depends largely upon the music of verse and "the use of language and metaphor lifted out of the common mould" (86). Lacking the incantational powers of poetic language and therefore much of the intensifying effect of poetry, the novel achieves its purpose by its breadth—by so representing the individual life as the product of external circumstances as to give it another kind of universality. The proper aim of the novel is not to represent individual character—this is the aim of epic and drama—but to represent the whole life of a people or of some phase of society. In the contemplation of this representation, the reader once again senses himself as part of a larger life than his own and experiences something of that illusion of freedom he derives from poetry's idealization of the individual will. As for lyric poetry, its function is also dualistic—to show both the charm and the illusory nature of the world.[8]

In this discussion of genres, More speaks as if drama were a species of poetry, ignoring the prose drama of modern literature. He regards the drama as essentially poetic in its intensity—its concentration and its emphasis on character—and he thinks that this intensity is best supported by poetic language. The modern prose drama, with its social and naturalistic tendencies, he apparently considered a moral and an esthetic lapse. For that matter, he saw signs that the novel too had reached its pinnacle and was now, in its naturalistic phase, in decline.[9]

This distinction More sees between poetry and prose is obviously not simply a matter of language: it is one of subject matter and depth of vision. And it is not particularly complimentary to the novelist. The value of a novel, More believes, depends chiefly on the intrinsic value of the national life or the phase of society it portrays and much less than the value of poetry on the skill of the writer. The novelist is far more subject to his environment than the poet, "for he deals less with the unchanging laws of character and more with what he perceives outwardly about him" (*SE*, III, 88-89). This distinction pretty well reflects More's tastes. Although he admired a number of novelists—Hawthorne and Trollope, for example—he thought poetry the higher form of art: "In a way the novel differs from poetry as photography differs from art."[10]

There is no point, however, in exaggerating the importance of these distinctions in More's criticism, for whether in poetry or in prose he is less concerned with formal considerations than with substantive. What is significant is that whatever formal distinctions he makes—few, undeveloped, and *a priori* as they may be—are dualist distinctions. "Works of art," he writes in "Definitions of Dualism,"

> are varied in so far as they are created by the imagination out of the material of the flux, and substantially they depend on the richness of the artist's experience. Formally they rise to a common standard of excellence in so far as the imagination of the artist is subject to the control of the unvaried inner check. So too, taste, or the appreciation of art, passes from the impressionistic whim of the individual and from the larger convention of an age or a people to a universal canon just to the degree that it is regulated by the inner check. Criticism is thus not left to waver without a fixed criterion; and in the understanding of dualism it possesses further a key to the main divergencies of thought and action, and a constant norm of classification. (*SE*, VIII, 264-65)

IV *Character*

Despite More's occasional reference to a cosmic or ontological dualism, his dualism is moral and psychological. The importance he attaches to conduct is apparent even in his literary standards: "art, so long as it is human, must concern itself with the portrayal of character—triumphant or defeated, still character—just as surely as religion is concerned with the creation of character" (*SE*, X, 303-4).

Occasionally we notice that it is fidelity to the tradition of moral responsibility which justifies, in More's eyes, many writers whom he might otherwise be inclined to reject. What, besides his style, saves Gissing "from insufferable dreariness" is that he presents "that last inviolable mystery of man's nature, the sense of personal responsibility" (*SE*, V, 58). Even the dreary poetry of seventeenth-century New England is made nobler in More's eyes by its devotion to character (*SE*, XI, 3-32). What makes English literature the greatest of modern literatures "despite its deficiencies of form and ideas," he says, is "the deep-rooted convention of moral responsibility" (*SE*, V, 59). To those who regard the moral tradition as narrow and provincial he retorts that, on the contrary, the narrow and provincial tradition is the tradition of non-morality (*SE*, X, 30).

He sees two general ways in which character and morality show themselves in literature. The first is formal: through the artist's practice of artistic restraint and discipline. The second and more obvious way is material: through the artist's acknowledgement, in his subject and theme, of the moral law. It may seem strange to see artistic control referred to as a moral quality, but in More's mind any restraint—any imposition of form—is moral. Artistic restraint—the restraint, say, of classical literature—is merely the working in art of the moral virtue. Thus, the failings of Wordsworth's poetry are essentially failings of character (*SE*, VII, 27-48). One of the esthetic principles of More's dualism is that we are pleased by the beauty of nature because we see it as the product of a force which is analogous to the inner check of our own consciousness (*SE*, VIII, 261-62); the beauty of literature depends on the presence of a similar quality. It is consciousness of dualism that distinguishes the genius from the mere man of talent (*SE*, VIII, 265); it is artistic restraint which distinguishes the better from the inferior work of poets like Longfellow (*SE*, V, 144-47) and Emerson (*SE*, XI, 85-87). Restraint and other qualities related to it are the *sine qua non* of literature. More grants the value, even the necessity, of the artist's use of raw, unformed material; but such material can be made into literature only by the addition of qualities he calls "aristocratic": form, reflection, discrimination, the transmutation of emotion into idea. "In a word, the aristocratic element denotes self-control, discipline, suppression" (*SE*, V, 28-29). One of the functions of the critic is to instill these qualities in the writer who does not already have them. The difference between poet and critic is that in the poet "the principle of restraint works unconsciously and from without," but in the critic "it proceeds consciously and from within" (*SE*, III, 73).

So far is More carried by his concern for restraint that he appears at times to be imposing on English literature a set of un-English criteria—at least to be regarding it from a somewhat un-English point of view. While he seems to accept Shakespeare's equality with Homer—"They rise together into the sky like the twin peaks of Parnassus, and in them the Old World and the New meet with equal and sufficient champions" (*SE*, II, 197)— he only *seems* to do so. For he very much regretted that English literature did not have, during its formative period in the Renaissance, some great critic like Boileau, backed if necessary by the power of the Crown as Boileau was backed by Louis XIV, to impose order and restraint upon the Elizabethan writers great and small—upon Shakespeare, Spenser, the sonneteers. "We should have had our own classics, and not been forced to turn to Athens for our canons of taste" (*SE*, III, 71-72). Shakespeare is cumulatively overwhelming, but he is savage and barbarous in both language and action; the tragedy of English literature is that "so great a genius so little disciplined" should have had such an influence upon it.[11]

More once listed the writers who had seemed most important to him personally as "Homer, Sophocles, Pindar, Plato, Virgil, Horace, Racine, Molière, Sainte-Beuve, Milton, Byron (the satire), Thackeray, and Matthew Arnold. You see that Shakespeare is out, and also all Spanish, Italian, and German authors."[12] He would later have added more English writers to the list: Johnson, Newman, Henry More, Henry Vaughan, and Trollope were among "the few who speak in a language I completely understand."[13] But they too are preponderantly classical or Platonic. These lists do not necessarily include all the writers More would have considered great, but they suggest the quality of his interest. What he was most drawn to in English literature was not the English tradition in any comprehensive sense—for that matter, who has such a catholic taste?—but the English branch of the classical or the classical branch of the English. "Homer wrote the only real poetry and there has been only imitation of him in a bungling sort of way ever since."[14]

It is understandable therefore that More should so much have loved the literature of the eighteenth century, when the exuberance of the Renaissance had given way to restraint, when enthusiasm and sectarianism had at least theoretically been tempered by common sense, when individualism and inspiration were chastened by constant reference to tradition. Probably the class of writers whom More most loves in English literature is the religious, of which Milton, Newman, Whittier, and Vaughan may serve as examples; after that, I believe, would come the neo-classical and Augustan writers of the eighteenth century. He had read Pope's *Epistle to Dr. Arbuthnot* "oftener, perhaps, than any other English poem except *Lycidas*" (*SE*, X, 140).

It is obvious, furthermore, that More's attraction to the eighteenth century is not merely a preference in reading matter, but that his literary standards are in many ways the standards of the eighteenth century. He extols temperance, restraint, decorum, and common sense; he forms his taste on tradition— even on the "Ancients"; he distrusts the exuberance of genius; he sees the artist as a teacher; he roots the distinctions between literary genres in nature; his conception of human nature is classically humanistic. In no way, perhaps, does he precisely echo the eighteenth century. His classicism is modified by his temperamental romanticism, by his personal religious and phil-osophical interests, and by the advantage of historical perspec-tive on the limitations of eighteenth century taste. But his kin-ship with the Augustans is too obvious to be overlooked.

Another aspect of More's concern with character is his interest in the character of the author—and here, perhaps, is another source of his attraction to the eighteenth century, which is so plentiful in letters, biography, and other revelations of character. He once explained, in regard to his admiration for Samuel Johnson, that "this fact of character, or personality, outweighs with me all other matters."[15] What More said of Sainte-Beuve is equally true of himself: "He might almost be accused of slighting the written word in order to get at the secret of the writer" (*SE*, III, 78).

Some of More's essays—"George Herbert" (*SE*, IV, 66-98) is an example—are biographical sketches illustrated from their sub-jects' works. By his own admission his essay on Hazlitt dwells "perhaps . . . too much on Hazlitt the man" (*SE*, II, 86) and not enough on the work, but he contends that with some authors the personality so dominates the work that to discuss the work is to discuss the man. The emphasis on character leads him at times into strange judgments on the work, and sometimes into strange uncertainties. After studying a six-volume edition of Swinburne for "several months," he must still admit to an uncertainty about the poems. He cannot tell whether they are sincere, and part of the reason is his "lack of biographical information" (*SE*, III, 100). Yet he nonetheless finishes his essay with his impressions of the man. In his essay on Shakespeare he reverses his procedure, turning the sonnets, whose sincerity he accepts, into auto-biography, and examining through them the "darker side of Shakespeare's character" (*SE*, II, 45). From the first volume of the *Shelburne Essays* to the last, one of his most persistent interests is the character of the author.

The biographical emphasis is to be expected in essays, like "The Correspondence of William Cowper" (*SE*, III, 1-27), which were originally reviews of biographies, memoirs, or correspond-ence. But not all of it can be so explained. Rather, to borrow his description of Hazlitt, More was chiefly interested in "that middle ground where life and literature meet, where life be-comes self-conscious through expression, and literature retains the reality of association with facts" (*SE*, III, 78). The most intimate meeting of literature and life, he believed, was in the man who wrote, seen through his writings.

V *The Personal Response*

Generally speaking, there are two types of writer who, by the standards of the *Shelburne Essays*, fall short of greatness. Some writers, who have an instinctive apprehension of dualism, have insufficient skill in expressing it. Others, who have undeniable skill, are kept from greatness by the insufficiency of their vision, by their misconceptions of life. More has a predilection for the former. While he admits that Whittier is largely commonplace (*SE*, III, 36) and that Swinburne stands "among the immortals of our pantheon," he "would surrender the wind-swept rhap-sodies of Swinburne for the homely conversation of Whittier" (*SE*, III, 123). The commonplace, he contends, is tolerable, even enjoyable in its sphere, but the false is noxious in propor-tion to the genius of its creator. The man whose taste is truly formed senses this distinction: "There is nothing mutually ex-clusive in the complete enjoyment of Milton and Crabbe; it is at least questionable whether the same man can heartily admire both Milton and Shelley" (*SE*, VII, 26). But while More's preferences in literature are motivated in part by his "invincible feeling that true art is in some way based on truth" (*SE*, X, 145), they spring equally from the fact that what he looks for in literature—and what he finds in the writers whom he most admires—is a correspondence to his own experience of things. "There are poets," he candidly admits, "who, by virtue of some affinity of spirit with our own, appeal to us with an intimacy that takes our judgement captive; we go to them in secret, so to speak, and love them beyond the warrant of our critical discernment" (*NSE*, I, 143).

The phrase "the homely conversation of Whittier" is a clue to the relationship that exists in the *Shelburne Essays* between Paul Elmer More and the author he is considering or between More and his reader. It does Lamb an injustice to treat his work as "literature great in any proper sense of the word" (*SE*, IV, 157); rather, we read him to meet him as a person and a friend—and "Charles Lamb Again" (*SE*, IV, 156-79) illustrates the point. More speaks of Donald G. Mitchell as "the companion who can beguile me through Europe with scraps of the classical poets we learned at school. . . . With so Virgilian a comrade I protest I can cross even the Channel without bickering. And how shall I quarrel with a friend who quotes Tacitus and Juvenal to me at Lyons; or at Vaucluse reminds me of 'some heart-killing Laura in his Homeland' in the language of Petrarch—*nelle medesime dolenti parole* . . . ?" (*SE*, V, 161-62).

More's statement that he rather likes Trollope's way of intruding into his novels to chat with the reader (*NSE*, I, 102) is another admission that literature is a personal communication between men of common interests. In his essay on Fanny Burney, More describes the great pleasure of writing about authors whom his readers and he both admire: "It is good to recall in solitude the speech and acts of a dear friend; it is good also to sit with one who has known him, and to talk over his generous ways" (*SE*, IV, 39). In fact, he hopes the *Shelburne Essays* will be "a dialogue in which the reader plays an equal part with the writer in cherishing the memory of great moments and persons of our literature" (*SE*, IV, 39-40).

In proportion as More personally enjoys the conversation of his cherished authors, so does he resent virtually as a personal affront the presumptions of many another. His "invincible prepossession" in favor of babblers and sentimental humorists who have written merely for his entertainment gives way to impatience with anyone who challenges him "to take a stand upon questions of fundamental veracity"—with "a Tolstoy, himself a compound of the humanitarian and the decadent, who cries out the Gospel of Jesus on the street corners, a Browning who imposes on the world as a spiritual teacher, a Swinburne who mouths the great words of liberty and righteousness" (*SE*, IV, 277). We often sense More's reluctance to give such writers his time. The beginning of his essay on Joyce suggests that he has been provoked into writing because of the necessity of defending his judgment. He had at first seen nothing worthwhile in Joyce, but he had been startled by T. S. Eliot's praise into reconsidering his opinion. He now admits the presence of certain beauties in Joyce, but his judgment is still on the whole unfavorable (*NSE*, III, 69-96). Although it might seem that writers like Tolstoy and Joyce, whatever their faults, would be infinitely more interesting than writers like Crabbe and Whittier, they are not so for More. He could grant that the achievement of Wordsworth and Shelley almost justifies their enormities (*SE*, III, 35), and he gives his attention to them. But he finds it more congenial to advance another function of criticism—"to set forth and as far as possible rescue from oblivion the inexhaustible entertainment of the lesser writers" (*SE*, VII, 26).

More responds to his reading with an intensity of emotion which is characteristic of response to vital rather than to vicarious experience—which is not, at least, to be described as critical detachment. There is an "execrable gust for blood," he protests, which "makes a good deal of Crashaw almost revolting to a healthy mind" (*SE*, VII, 165). In a tone of shocked disbelief he hopes that Lamb has exaggerated somewhat in his account of a two-day debauch with Coleridge (*SE*, II, 92). He must justify his liking for Milton's poetry because there is so much to object to in the poet's character (*NSE*, III, 186-92). Yet these are writers toward whom he is favorably disposed; toward others he is a good deal less charitable, especially when he finds any unwholesomeness of their character transmitted to their works. Portions of the essay "Decadent Wit" (*SE*, X, 279-304), on Oscar Wilde and his circle, show More so overcome by his reaction to "license and disease" (301) as to appear incapable of detecting the value of a work. He can reduce *Crime and Punishment* to the following summation: "Somehow we are to be lifted up by sympathizing with a madman worshipping humanity in the person of a girl of the street. Filth, disease, morbid dreams, bestiality, insanity, sodden crime, these are the natural pathway to the emancipation of the spirit . . ." (300).

In the *New Shelburne Essays* such denunciation becomes almost a reflex action whenever More finds himself in the presence of contemporary literature. In "James Joyce," for example, he quotes a passage from the section in *Ulysses* in which Bloom attends Paddy Dignam's funeral:

> An obese grey rat toddled along the side of the crypt, moving the pebbles. An old stager: great-grandfather: he knows the ropes. The grey alive crushed itself in under the plinth, wriggling itself in under it. Good hidingplace for treasure.[16]

"There is worse than that," More comments, "much worse; things that the normal human mind would never imagine and that it would be a pollution to quote" (*NSE*, III, 91). Many readers have found "worse than that" in *Ulysses*, but worse than *that* need not be very bad.

More's vehement reaction to sordid material, and particularly to any amoral presentation of immorality, is what gives rise to the charge of prudery which is occasionally raised against him. Yet he once objected himself that the editor of an edition of Walpole's letters had included "the most insignificant scraps of correspondence" while suppressing "more vital passages . . . which might offend a prudish taste" (*SE*, IV, 255). Again, speaking of Laurence Sterne's imputed immorality, More asks: ". . . in all honesty, are we not prone to fall into cant whenever this topic is broached?" Though both Sterne and Rabelais deliberately depict "the under side of human nature" in order "to show how Fortune smiles at the social proprieties," no harm can come "to a mature mind" from either writer; even the immature are more likely to be corrupted by *Venus and Adonis* and by other works like it "which throw the colours of a glowing imagination over what is in itself perfectly natural and wholesome." If Sterne is objectionable, he is so on grounds of taste rather than on grounds of morality: "He merely erred at times by excess of method" (*SE*, III, 206-8).

On occasion what appears to be mere prudishness in the *Shelburne Essays* is a scruple about artistic propriety. Balzac's description of Eugénie Grandet, for example, has "a freshness and chastity not common in his books, or, indeed, appropriate to most of his women." For that very reason there is an artistic defect, a failure in *artistic* prudence, in his insinuating "how she would have appealed to the Parisian roué." The reader, More believes, is not likely to distinguish what is ascribed to the woman by the author from what is merely said about her in explanation of someone else's possible reaction, and is therefore in danger of deriving from Balzac's description an impression which the author does not intend to convey (*SE*, V, 80).

But if More is not prudish, he certainly is squeamish. Of the sexual license of the Restoration theater he observes, quoting Charles Lamb, "It is pleasant enough, no doubt, now and then 'to take an airing beyond the diocese of the strict conscience,' and there may be a healthy relaxation in getting at times into a complete 'privation of moral light'—if it were n't for the odour! The smell of the thing in that darkness cannot be concealed; the very reek and noisomeness of it prevent you from walking there for long as in a place of immaterial fancy" (*SE*, X, 77-78). More is sensitive about other kinds of immorality too. *The Adventures of Tom Sawyer,* he believes, is "the most notable example" of a "class of children's books which are not only enfeebling in their effect on the mind, but actually perverting in their effect on character." Tom's exploits are undeniably comical, but he is an idealization of "the victorious liar, lucky vagabond, cunning rebel to authority."[17]

But the immorality which More most objects to, the most serious offense an artist can commit, is not the obvious one of obscenity or suggestiveness, but a falsification of human nature, the denial of moral responsibility. This falsification is both a moral and an artistic failing. Beaumont and Fletcher, for example, in failing to depict the central restraining faculty of the soul and in making their plays conflicts of passion only, represent human nature as "a mere bundle of unrelated instincts." Yet so closely interrelated are moral judgment and intellectual comprehension that the "incomprehensible tangle of passions" of *The Maid's Tragedy* weakens our sympathetic response to "the exquisite painting of the emotions" and leaves finally a "blurred impression in memory." The profounder pleasure which derives from greater art—from *Romeo and Juliet* or *Hippolytus*—comes from an intimate union of emotion and understanding: "We understand a thing as we see a principle of unity at work within or behind a changing group of appearances" (*SE*, X, 20-21).

Few of us rise above our temperaments, and if More's tastes— undoubtedly a bit squeamish by the standards of our day—occasionally obtrude, we should keep two things in mind. One is that the moral standard he defends and applies has been the most generally applied criterion of literary value in English criticism from the beginning. The other is that a moral standard, even though there is much more in literature than morality, is no more likely to be misapplied than any other. Furthermore, despite an occasional instance of excessive moralism, More's application of the standard is discriminating and generous. No criticism is likely to deal with all aspects of a work or a literature. More chose for his object the elucidation of a certain tradition in English literature and more generally in Western culture. It is true that he defines that tradition rather exclusively by moral standards. "To belittle . . . the importance of ethical truth in literature," he writes, "is to surrender the most decisive instrument in the hands of the critic" (*SE*, X, 75). Nevertheless, his criticism should be judged by its best accomplishment, of which the essays on Hawthorne and Poe, Crabbe, Whitman, Thoreau's journal, Gissing, Chesterfield, Sir Thomas Browne, and Jonathan Edwards—and, in the *New Shelburne Essays*, those on Vaughan and *Lycidas*—will serve as examples.[18]

VI *Sir Thomas Browne and Whitman*

Not all of the *Shelburne Essays* contain all of the elements I have been describing here; among those that do contain all or nearly all, there is a variety of pattern dictated by the requirements of individual subject and theme. "Sir Thomas Browne" (*SE*, VI, 154-86) will serve as a typical example. Beginning with a short summary of the author's life, it proceeds to a somewhat longer survey of his writings, describes and illustrates the intellectual temper of the seventeenth century, shows how that temper is reflected in Browne's works, describes his individual achievement and the quality of his mind, places these in the context of the philosophical tradition of the West, analyzes his most important works with particular attention to his prose style, and concludes with an appraisal of his character. Throughout,

More makes constant use of dualism—but he does so naturally enough, since the essay is one of the pieces in *Studies of Religious Dualism.*

In more detail, the essay reads as follows. Sir Thomas Browne was influenced to an unusual degree by a single idea which dominated his age—the idea that man's whole conception of the universe must be reconstituted along the lines laid down by abstract reason and physical science. Although he contributed intellectually to the forwarding of this idea, he was temperamentally a reactionary; his *Pseudodoxia* is a reflection of the paradox, being primarily an antiquarian amassing of citations and only secondarily a scientific exposure of error. His religion is similarly paradoxical. Although it was of a different sort from the responses which men like Pascal and Bunyan made to the rationalizing and deistic tendencies of the age, and one which they would hardly have recognized as Christian, it was nonetheless a true religion.

At this point, in order to illustrate further the qualities of Browne's religion, which More takes to be his peculiar achievement, More digresses into the relationship that exists between the religious or poetic imagination and the scientific imagination and then into the unlikely possibility, illustrated by a discussion of Lucretius and Newton, of their co-existing in the same mind. Browne, he concludes, "is one of the purest examples of the religious imagination severed from religious dogma or philosophy; dualism with him takes the form of an omnipresent and undefined mystery involving, and sometimes dissolving, the fabric of the world" (172). There lies a danger in Browne's romantic wonder which would come to a head in a later day, but his own character and the still vital tradition of religion saved him; he interpreted the law of nature by the law of the spirit.

Next follows a discussion of Browne's prose style—a mixture of Anglo-Saxon plainness and outlandish Latinity, florid and verbose at its worst, melodious and ecstatic at its best—and then the concluding remarks on the ambiguities and charms of Browne's character: his disillusionment and melancholy; his aloofness from the political quarrels of his times; his learning; his peculiar balance of wordly activity and religious quietude, of the scientific and the visionary; his tolerance and friendliness. If we knew Browne better, More is certain, we should find in the man himself the contentment we find in his works; he was "one of the few happy men of this world" (182). If we had the diary, now lost, which he apparently kept for himself, "we should the more abundantly admire the miracle of his daily life" (185).

More's essay on Whitman is in some ways similar; in others, not. It shows again More's emphasis upon a key trait of character, his reading of the writer's life in his works, and his linking of the author to a larger tradition. But while the larger tradition in which Browne is placed extends back into the history of religion and philosophy to Lucretius and St. Augustine as well as laterally into the Europe of the seventeenth century, Whitman's context is the literary context of the nineteenth century. Like the essay on Browne, this one also makes use of dualism but applies it less explicitly. Finally, while it reveals More's preference for conservative and classical standards in literature, it also shows—and perhaps it is most interesting for this reason— the balance and sensitivity of his treatment of an author whose personality he found largely repugnant. I conclude this analysis of the *Shelburne Essays* with a somewhat extensive summary of "Walt Whitman" (*SE*, IV, 180-211), in which I include, as illustration of More's tone and style, frequent and lengthy quotations from the essay.

Like a number of essays More first published as reviews, "Walt Whitman" begins with some brief comments on the works under review, in this instance biographical writings by several of Whitman's disciples, and then moves off into an argument of its own. One of the difficulties of coming to Whitman, More believes, is that the reader must first disengage himself from the idolatry of the poet's admirers. The best commentary on Whitman's life is *Specimen Days*, and the most meaningful aspect of that work is its revelation of Whitman's fascination with the flow, the roll, the sweep of things: "It was always the tides of life that attracted him" (189-90). But just as in his jottings on the war he noted, beneath "the physical impression of endlessly marching troops, of interminable shadowy processions through the lonely roads of Virginia and in the streets of Washington," the great unison of men in a common purpose, so there came to Whitman himself "a deepening and purifying of his nature" (191) and an insight into the unity that underlies the flux.

The return to nature, which Whitman saw as the only cure for immorality and the distractions of civilization and toward which, he believed, all true religion and literature pointed, required of him a violation of poetic convention. Looking upon the rhythm and spirit of conventional verse as anachronisms which deprived the poet of his freedom and insulated him from the currents of life, Whitman returned "to the liquid abandon of the waves and the winds" (193). Unfortunately, in breaking with conventions that were in fact largely a sham, he often forgot other conventions which originate in the demands of human nature. Too many of his poems are a preaching on poetry rather than a writing of it. A comparison between him and a dozen or more other poets who also sought to revivify the form and spirit of poetry shows him a second best. He is inferior at any point of comparison with Arnold, Wordsworth, Landor, Longfellow, Shelley, Gray, or Byron; he preached what these others did.

On the other hand, when he forgets his doctrine and turns to inspiration, he shows himself a true poet. Single lines can evoke the image or memory of subtle sounds and odors. An occasional phrase condenses a system of morals into an epigram. Paragraphs "hold the true poetic emotion and stand out from their context like those half-evolved figures of Rodin struggling from their matrix" (199). Some short poems are worthy of any anthology; long ones now and then display a grandiose but stumbling craftsmanship. In these successful passages Whitman's rhythms are not so lawless as he and his supporters have supposed. "Whispers of heavenly death murmur'd I hear" is certainly not his best work, but it compares well with Browning's "Prospice" and Tennyson's "Crossing the Bar." Browning's lines are in substance the crude individualism of a man who sees only his personal emotions, which he would take, if he could, into the grave; Tennyson's "luminous throbbing image" merges the soul into "the great tides of being from whence it sprung" (202) and makes of the personality a mystic symbol. But Whitman, though he posed as a rank egotist, shows less of egotism in the presence of death than either of these contemporaries:

> Here all thought of self is lost in a vague rapport, as he would say, with the dim suggestions of whispering, cloud-wrapped night; here is a perception of spiritual values far above the anthropomorphism of Browning, and a power of evoking a poetical mood, when once we have trained our ear to bring out his rhythms, as strong, though not as permanent, as Tennyson's.

In this note of almost pantheistic revery, the lines may represent a departure from Whitman's earlier manner, but in another respect they exhibit the most constant and characteristic of his qualities—the sense of ceaseless indistinct motion, intimated in the sound of ascending footsteps and of the unseen flowing rivers, expressed more directly in the shifting clouds and the far off appearing and disappearing star. (202-3)

And this is the impression that Whitman finally leaves—an impression of indiscriminate motion, of solid momentous realities "filled with blind portents for the soul" (203). The observer seems now to be moving through a cluster of objects beheld momentarily vividly and then lost, and again standing stationary as visions throng past him. In either case he has been merged in vast unbroken processions that begin and end beyond the reaches of time. Whitman never forgot the motion of the sea, the rush of ferries, the pulsations of Broadway. Life for him was an Open Road, a long climb, through the past, up the infinite gradations of time—and in the future an unending voyage, an unfolding cosmic purpose:

> To most men, when their eyes within are opened, that spectacle brings a feeling of painful doubt. The mere physical perception of innumerable multitudes jostling forward with no apparent goal, contains an element of intellectual bewilderment for the observer. His own identity is suddenly threatened, and the meaning of his existence becomes as obscure to him as that of the alien individualities that crowd his path. And when this spectacle, as it does with some men, passes into an intuition of vast shadowy fluctuations in the invisible world, the bewilderment grows to a sense of terror, even of despair. It is the tonic quality of Whitman—the quality for which his sane readers return to him again and again—that his eyes were opened to this vision, and that he remained unafraid. All the vociferousness of his earlier poems is little more than a note of defiance against the thronging shapes that beset him. But I think it was something more than his obstreperous individualism that saved him in the end. Look into his face, especially in the noble wartime picture of him called the Hugo portrait, and you will be struck by that veiled brooding regard of the eyes which goes with the vision of the seer. He felt not only his personal identity entrenched behind walls of inexpugnable egotism, but he was conscious, also, of another kind of identity, which made him one with every living creature, even with the inanimate ele-

ments. He was no stranger in the universe. The spirit that gazed out of his own eyes into the unresting multitude looked back at him with silent greeting from every passing face. And it was chiefly through this higher identity, or sympathy, that he cast away fear. (205-6)

While it is supposed that Whitman relegated all former religions and literatures to oblivion and inaugurated a new civilization, he always avoided programs; for all his vaunted democracy, he offers little practical help to reformers. Even more than Emerson's is his philosophy a fraternal anarchy in which there is little room for obligations of family or state. He formed in his life no exclusive friendships; his universe of ceaseless motion reveals neither time nor place for enduring unions. But there came with the war "the first note of that deeper mysticism which looks through the illusions of change into the silence of infinite calm" (208); his daily contact with death was the last stage in his initiation:

> To that diviner glimpse [of the gods who sit beyond the curtain of death] Whitman never quite attained, and this is well, for in attaining it he would have passed beyond the peculiar inspiration which makes him what he is. . . .
> He lacked the rare and unique elevation of Emerson from whom so much of his vision was unwittingly derived, but as a compensation his temperament is richer than the New England poet's, and his verbal felicity at its best more striking. I do not see why Americans should hesitate to accept him, with all his imperfections and incompleteness, and with all his vaunted pedantry of the pavement, as one of the most original and characteristic of their poets. . . . (210-11)

CHAPTER 3

Justice and Reform

D URING HIS EDITORSHIP of the *Nation* and on into the 1920's, More was perhaps as well known for his political conservatism as for his literary criticism; possibly he is still so known.[1] Some of his utterances—*"the rights of property are more important than the right to life"* (*SE*, IX, 136)—have to the liberal ear of the middle twentieth century as odious a sound as Michael Wigglesworth's stanzas on the damnation of unbaptized infants had to More's (*SE*, XI, 13). Others have the sound of rant, either because we have long since become accustomed to the institutions and habits of mind against which they were directed or because they were directed against fads which are no longer current. As I have already said, his social and political writings, more than his literary criticism, are a response to the events of his times. On the assumption that these writings will be better understood if seen against the background of events, the present chapter surveys in some detail the social and political climate of the late nineteenth and the early twentieth centuries.

I *The Impact of Darwin*

The most important intellectual development of the late nineteenth century in America was the general acceptance of Darwin's evolutionary hypothesis in biology and the extension of evolutionary theories into philosophy, religion, and the social sciences.[2] Largely because it seemed to conflict with the religious conception that God had created the universe in a series of distinct acts, the Darwinian hypothesis found slow acceptance among naturalists; even so, by the late 1870's it dominated their thinking. The universities followed the scientists, and the press had reported on evolution from the beginning. It was not long, therefore, before evolutionary theories had received such widespread dissemination and acceptance throughout all levels of American society as to make the United States, as Richard Hofstadter remarks, "*the* Darwinian country" (4). By the end of the century, evolution was such a fad that adherents of various programs and positions, including many who had at first most strongly opposed it, were appealing to it for their authority.

First to appropriate it for non-scientific purposes were defenders of economic laissez faire, who appealed to the law of nature they found in Darwin and his popularizers to justify economic individualism and to argue that change in society should be as unhurried and spontaneous as change in nature. The gospel of wealth, as their doctrine was often called, held that the governance of society, particularly in economics, should be entrusted to a natural élite whose very survival in the competitive struggle was evidence of their superiority. Although it rested also on more traditional supports—on the popular notion that those who risked most should profit most, on the Protestant conception of an earthly calling, and on the classical economics of Adam Smith and James Mill—its evolutionary support became increasingly important as Protestantism and classical economics declined in prestige toward the close of the century. Indeed, though economic and social reformers also used evolutionary arguments, the term "social Darwinism" refers primarily to the evolutionary defense of laissez faire.

The decline in the prestige of the Protestant Churches was brought on in part by a rationalist criticism of their theology and in part by the real or supposed connections which existed between Protestantism and the gospel of wealth. Since the time of the Civil War the urban working class had become increasingly indifferent to the Churches, which were generally middle class and tended to ignore the evils of urban poverty and industrialism. To combat this indifference, a number of Protestant leaders in the 1870's extended the social activities of their Churches beyond the usual anti-vice campaigns into philanthropic and educational work. This was the beginning of the social gospel movement, which through the closing years of the nineteenth century and into the opening of the twentieth took an increasing interest in the cause of labor and in social reform. What leaders of the movement sought was the social application of religious principles, and before long a number of Churches and inter-Church organizations not only were attacking the ethics of industrial society, but were openly supporting the labor movement. In 1903 both the Methodist Baltimore General Council and the Federal Council of Churches of Christ in America published statements on social reform which anticipated the Progressive Party platform of 1912.

The social gospel was brought about in large part by a conciliation between the Protestant churches and two forces which had seemed at first to threaten them. One of these was the so-called "higher criticism" of the Bible; the other consisted of a number of developments in the physical sciences, and chiefly in biology and geology, of which Darwin's work was the most impressive. The higher criticism, a method of scientific and historical analysis of biblical texts which was brought to this country from Germany toward the end of the nineteenth century, questioned the authenticity of theological miracles and revelation as well as the historicity of biblical texts, suggesting that Christianity rested on a mere compilation of primitive myths. The physical sciences seemed to support the higher criticism. Sir Charles Lyell in geology had shown the earth to be considerably older than its supposed six thousand or so years; and when Darwin posited a universe governed by chance and hereditary determination, it seemed to some as if Christianity had been entirely discredited.

But Asa Gray, the leading American botanist of the time, had argued since the *Origin of Species* had first appeared that Darwin's hypothesis was compatible with both atheism and theism, and it was not long after evolution had become generally accepted in biology that preachers and theologians were coming to look upon it as in itself a manifestation of providence. Henry Ward Beecher called himself a Christian evolutionist; Lyman Abbott and Washington Gladden described Christianity as a product of evolutionary development. By showing that God was Himself evolving His purpose in the world, the identification of evolution with providence supported those churchmen who would broaden the social and secular activities of the Churches. A similar meeting, with a similar result, took place between the Churches and the higher criticism. Although it denied the supernatural element in the Scriptures, the higher criticism offered the alternative conception of a completely human Christ Whose promised kingdom was an earthly one. It was this conception of Christ as the epitome of God's love at work in the world upon which the leaders of the social gospel seized in the early twentieth century to give their program what seemed a more realistic and historical basis than had been provided in the nineteenth century by the vaguer idealistic notions of Christian stewardship then in vogue.

So far did the Churches go in their social concerns that American Protestantism lost some of its animosity toward socialism. While suspecting both the theory and practical efficiency of socialism, early leaders of the social gospel admitted the truth of its description of economic evils; stimulated by a desire to forestall it, they took from it a number of its more moderate aims. As time passed, preachers like George Herron and Walter Rauschenbusch went further, either joining the Socialist Party or establishing socialist programs and organizations of their own. In 1909 the periodical *Christian Socialist* claimed two thousand clergymen among its subscribers and at one point ran special issues featuring spokesmen from the various denominations.

It was at this stage in the development of modern American society, when the influence of Darwin had spread into all sectors of American intellectual life and the Protestant Churches, largely reconciled to both Darwinism and higher criticism, were on their way to some formal adoption of reform, that More began his attack upon the compound enemy of scientism and humanitarianism. The high point of his assault was the publication of *Aristocracy and Justice* in 1915, but he made constant sallies over the full extent of his career[3] and engaged the enemy in all its forms—the Darwinian hypothesis pure and simple, together with its offshoots in modern psychology, humanitarian literature and art, pragmatism, progressivism, socialism, and humanitarian religion. Indeed, More professed in the beginning to regard the religious aspect of the movement as the essential one: "We are not Christians, but humanitarians, following a maimed and materialistic faith."[4]

II *Humanitarian Religion*

One of the earliest of More's criticisms is "The Religious Grounds of Humanitarianism" (*SE*, I, 225-53). Ostensibly a review of William Mallock's *Aristocracy and Evolution* (1892), which argues that the great man rather than the social group is the true cause of social progress, it is only incidentally concerned with Mallock's book. Mallock is right so far as he goes, says More, but he does not consider "the religious or humanitarian instinct of man" (227), on which the claims of socialism, Marxian or Christian, rest. The basic error of humanitarianism is that it confuses the religious instinct with worldly policy. The secular virtues are prudence, courage, and honor in the individual character, and justice, mercy, charity, and temperance for the well-being of society. The religious virtues, on the other hand, are faith, hope and love for the purely spiritual life, and humility, non-resistance, poverty, and chastity for where the spiritual meets the temporal. But these latter are negative, unworldly, and socially sterile, as we would expect from Christ's insistence that His kingdom is not of this world; to use them to regulate the temporal affairs of men leads both to a desecration of religion and to an unsettling of the social order. Faith, hope, and the golden rule are no substitute for prudence, courage, and honor; the evils of economic competition are more likely to be corrected by a better understanding and observation of the worldly virtues than by the sickly yearning of sentimentalists.

Less philosophical than the essay on Mallock, *The Jessica Letters,* which More admitted was "a medium wherein to vomit forth all my rage against humanitarianism,"[5] is also more sweeping and personal, naming some of the prominent reformers of the day and presenting in a less formal manner many of the author's opinions. One of its targets is Lyman Abbott—pastor of Plymouth Congregational Church in Brooklyn, editor of *The Outlook,* Christian evolutionist, and reformer—whose contention that service to man is the best service to God is to More a sham of true religion. Another is Jane Addams, of Hull House, whom he mentions elsewhere too. In *The Jessica Letters* he maintains that her insistence on the need for a code and practice of social morality is a rejection of the personal morality of traditional religion; in 1914 in "The New Morality" (*SE,* IX, 193-217), More bolsters this contention with a historical analysis. When during the Enlightenment, he writes, the sense of personal morality disappeared with the God of orthodox Christianity, the philosophes attributed human ills to the inhibitions of a corrupt society. Liberate human nature through the reform of institutions, they said, and men, following their instincts, will be good; let sympathy take the place of judgment. Despite the modern reformer's pretense of originality, and despite his repudiation of the vagueness and impracticality of the old idealists, there is little difference between the economics of Hull House and the ethics of Helvetius. But while religion once resisted the humanitarian ideal of personal irresponsibility, that resistance has largely disappeared; humanitarianism has itself become a religion which even the Churches have joined. Nevertheless, it will inevitably weaken the character of man; we cannot identify sympathy and justice except by nourishing the passions at the expense of the intellect and the will.

More was sufficiently concerned over the social gospel to address himself directly to it. "The Church and Politics" (*NSE*, III, 144-59), first published in 1934, considers the supposed obligation of the Church toward the redemption of society, the possibility of an earthly realization of the heavenly kingdom, and the flirtation of the Churches with socialism. Society, More admits, is in need of redemption, and the Church has a role in redeeming it. But he insists that the role is not political. For that matter, the equalitarianism of the socialists is an impossible ideal, since it slurs over the fact of human depravity; love has never conquered man's impulse to aggrandizement; and the events of the past twenty years indicate that men cannot effectually govern themselves. If the Church is to redeem society, it must carry on its traditional mission, preaching an eschatological rather than a sociological redemption. It is neither the sentiment of love nor any other sympathetic force that will mitigate the passions of men, but a sense of the soul's obligation to a supernatural power. If the Church cannot reinstill such a sense, the ideal of brotherhood will lead to an anti-religious state governed by those with a more realistic appraisal of the nature of man.

III *Pragmatism*

The desire for reform did not work through the Churches only. In the years following the Civil War there appeared, along with and even antedating the social gospel, a tendency to rely on purely human energies to make good the promises of democracy. Though it is commonly referred to as the religion of humanity, it was never an organized movement but included a number of parties and programs whose common mark was their distrust of religious orthodoxy. Its most prominent representatives were the Free Religious Association of Octavius B. Frothingham, founded in 1867, and the atheistic humanism of Robert G. Ingersoll. A related tendency, but one that is more important because it contributed directly to the political and economic reform of the Progressive Era, is seen in the work of Lester Ward, Edward Bellamy, and Henry George, who also grounded reform in science rather than religion and who chose the state rather than the Churches as their instrument. Each of these men had to grapple with Darwinism. Ward admitted the importance of biological selection but argued that the human mind could break out of the crude and wasteful process of biological development and mold nature to its own advantage. George and Bellamy maintained that Spencer's views of human development, which stressed the slowness and gradualness of biological change, were inadequate and fatalistic. Modern conditions called for radical changes, and cooperation rather than competition was needed to effect them. But before long the reformers had ceased to quarrel with Darwinism, for they had appropriated it for their own uses.

The conciliation of Darwinism and reform was brought about through new conceptions of the relationship that existed between organism and environment. While Spencerian psychology had emphasized the primacy of environment in producing biological changes, the pragmatists—after 1900 the dominant school in American psychology—stressed the ability of human beings to change their environment. In the new psychology, consciousness was no mere passive receptor but an instrument by which the human organism selected the proper means for satisfying its wants. The mind and its environment were constantly evolving in relation to each other. It was this conception, that consciousness is not an independent realm of being but a function of an organism, that Dewey took from William James and used as the basis of his work.[6] In giving the new psychology the status of a positive science and in making it independent of philosophy, James contributed enormously to the prestige and effectiveness of the reformers. Dewey credited him with being the progenitor of the whole Chicago school of instrumentalism.[7] More maintains, in "The Pragmatism of William James" (*SE*, VII, 195-212), that James's philosophy was self-contradictory from the start

and remained so through all the changes James worked upon it;
it was a rationalist attack upon rationalism. James, he predicted
elsewhere, would some day be found to be "among the dis-
integrating and deteriorating forces of the age" (*SE*, XI, 159).
More's treatment of Dewey, however, makes a more specific
connection between pragmatism and those forces.

Like Lester Ward, Dewey saw an opposition between the
evolutionary process, which is one of conflict, competition, and
struggle, and the ideals of human life, which are harmony and
community of well-being and which competition, he believed,
could hardly establish. But his conception of consciousness
enabled him to reconcile the two. Mind, he said, is both the
most advanced product of biological evolution and the organ by
which man can control his environment. In addition, he had a
conviction of the obligation of philosophy to apply the findings
of modern science to social life, and he called for a shift in
the attention of philosophers from metaphysics and epistemology
—sterile subjects, he thought—to politics, education, and morality.
This was the argument of *Reconstruction in Philosophy*.

From the beginning, according to Dewey, there were two
kinds of knowledge—religious beliefs, which arose out of primitive
man's fear of natural forces, and common-sense observations of
nature. Out of this second type of knowledge, science was
eventually to come; but because of its mundane and common
quality, it was relegated to an inferior position by the priests
and the higher classes whose interests lay in the other. As the
more acute minds of the educated grew disenchanted with superstition and gradually evolved philosophy, philosophy in its turn
became the ally of status and social prestige and looked askance
at the useful and the material. Philosophy thus became divorced
from a concern with contemporary needs; but if it were to serve
modern man as it ought to, it had to surrender its barren interests
in absolutes and support the attainment of social happiness.

The intellectual mission of the twentieth century, Dewey
argues, is to apply experimentation and invention to the social
order. Having learned that the human organism can change its
environment, having learned that reason need not work only with
inherited knowledge but can experiment and contrive as well,
we require a reconstructed philosophy which will make reality
conform to human ideals. In logic, the test of truth must be
effectiveness; the hypothesis that works is the true one. In

ethics, we must abandon the assumption of a single, final, and ultimate law of right and wrong in favor of a pragmatic morality which sees that situations are unique, that each has its own good and its own principle.

Reconstruction in Philosophy appeared in 1920. In 1921 More gave an address on "Religion and Social Discontent" (*NSE*, III, 117-43) at Lake Forest College; it was largely a discussion of Dewey's book, but it was also another denunciation of humanitarianism in general. This time, however, More contended not that humanitarianism was an inverted religion, but that it was essentially anti-religious, a variety of revolutionary atheism. It is a new materialism in full flourish that he sees in Dewey; and in making his point he emphasizes the evolutionary nature of Dewey's thought, stresses the anti-religious and anti-philosophical bias of his book, reduces Dewey's rationalism to sentimentalism, and labels meliorism a destructive force.

The truth is, More admits, that religion has been a conservative and regulatory force in human affairs. Those who believe in the truth of religion regard its social effects as beneficial; the materialists and skeptics are divided, with some finding it a valid instrument for social control and others maintaining that it inhibits progress. The quarrel goes back at least to the Enlightenment, but it has recently been aggravated by the intrusion of "the great and all-devouring doctrine of evolution" (125). Dewey's argument is simple. Progress is measured by the satisfaction of material wants, and effort toward material production depends upon dissatisfaction with present conditions. Religion, because it allays discontent, inhibits progress. Thus, says More, the matter hinges on the relative merits of religious contentment and social discontent. The former is a compound of humility and meekness; the latter is that "perpetual and restless desire of power after power" which Hobbes described as the general condition of mankind in a state of nature. Social life could not continue if all men came for even a short time under the exclusive influence of one of these principles. Recognizing this fact, religion upholds the ideals of humility and meekness but allows men to live under the normal conditions of the world. The materialists, in contrast, can admit no standard but their own. To them religious peace is cowardice, sham, and the foe of progress—something that must be destroyed in order that material values no longer be confused.

Yet the materialist does not want the cruelty and warfare of Hobbes's state of nature: "It is rather the mark of modern naturalism that it is plastered up and down, swathed and swaddled, masked and disguised, with sentimentalisms" (137). Once we have set our minds to the production of comfort, we are told by Dewey and his kind, we shall achieve a universal state of brotherhood. "Sympathy, they maintain, is a natural instinct of the heart, . . . and of itself will control the other natural instincts if unhampered by false ideals" (138). History shows the error of such a belief, although the reformers are correct in their other point: progress does come from social discontent. The difficulty is that when progress is measured by material standards only and when no supernatural hope is offered as compensation for the disappointments of this life, there is nothing to resist the blind craving for power after power. Stripped of its sentimentality, this belief in social progress is the law of the jungle, and its preachers are instilling into society a discontent which, being impossible to satisfy, will engender hatred and distrust and end in the destruction of civilized life.

"Religion and Social Discontent" is a continuation of the argument of "The New Morality" of seven years before, and More is right in seeing Dewey and Jane Addams as the same opponent. Jane Addams spoke from the point of view of a social worker, and the sentimentality of her appeal is evident in her language; Dewey's position is that of a philosopher concerned with intellectual and moral integrity. Yet both call for a flexible, socially oriented ethical standard, and both insist that melioration of social evils is one of the highest purposes of democracy. Dewey's importance in the intellectual and social history of the United States in the twentieth century is quite evident today. Herbert W. Schneider calls him "the chief American exponent and patron saint of democratic socialism" (566), and Eric Goldman's description of his influence sums up practically the entire movement of social reform we have been discussing:

Here was a philosophy and psychology perfectly tailored to progressive needs. From Henry George to Charles Beard, reform thinkers had been feeling their way toward specific pragmatisms in their own fields. In religion, economics, morals, criminology, anthropology, law, history, and political science, each had denied that the prevailing ideas could be eternally true, fixed by the nature of man and the universe. Each had insisted that conservatism be tested by its political, economic, and social results. Applying the test and finding conservatism wanting, each had proposed substantially the same change in ideas. Clergymen or economists, anthropologists or lawyers, reform thinkers wanted to replace an evolution that stopped at the present with an evolution that raced on; an environment that predetermined men and women with an environment that human beings manipulated to meet their needs; the dreary inevitabilities of Conservative Darwinism with the radiant hopefulness of Reform Darwinism. And now John Dewey had swept all their specific pragmatisms into a system from which each reformer, working away in his own field, could draw comfort and strength. (158-59)

More regarded Dewey as "perhaps the most influential teacher in America today" (*NSE*, III, 123), but in 1921 he could not quite have had Goldman's perspective; nor did he explicitly connect Dewey with progressivism. Yet More's treatment of progressivism, we shall presently see, shows that he saw both it and pragmatism as being equally products of humanitarianism and evolutionary thought.

IV *Science*

When More spoke of humanitarianism as at the same time scientific and sentimental, he was neither being paradoxical nor referring to separate halves of the movement. The scientific mind, he believed, was almost predisposed toward sentiment. Science, he says in "Huxley" (*SE*, VIII, 193-244), is "the observation and classification of facts and the discovery of those constant sequences in phenomena which can be expressed in mathematical formulae or in the generalized language of law" (193); but science tells us nothing of any purpose behind what it observes. In systematizing all those scientific observations which showed that plant and animal life had developed over the course of time from the simplest to the most complex of organisms, Darwin established a scientific law. When he sought to explain his law by a theory of natural selection, he went beyond positive science to an illicit use of scientific hypothesis. Hypothesis, More admits, has a proper place in science; but those who use it tend, like Darwin, to pass beyond it into philosophical or, as More calls it elsewhere, "ontological" (*SE*, VIII, 269-70) or metaphysical science. No matter how skeptical the scientist is when he advances his hypothesis, he almost always becomes convinced that his formulation of causes is as objectively real as the phenomena he is trying to explain.

Generally speaking, the scientist is safe as long as he restricts himself to the realm of nature. But nature is not the whole of experience, and a difficulty arises when the scientist confronts a body of evidence to the existence of a world of the inner life which is not governed by the mechanical regularity of nature. He can deny the evidence on the grounds that science cannot verify it and thereby deny all that the Christian believes. But if he finds it too insistent to deny, he is likely to broaden his hypothesis to include it. This is precisely what happened after Darwin. The impressiveness of Darwin's work and the simplicity of his theory led to the imposition of the evolutionary hypothesis on education, morality, religion, and government until it seemed as if the last mystery of being had been dissolved. Gradually, however, men recovered from their awe, and philosophical science has more lately taken another turn. It now attempts, while preserving the facts of evolution, to change the evolutionary hypothesis so as to include the spontaneous aspects of human nature under it. This attempt has had at least one interesting issue. During the nineteenth century there appeared to be an unalterable opposition between science and romanticism, but the two have now been merged. In place of Thomas Huxley, we have Bergson and William James.

The orthodox view of man that prevailed in the seventeenth century, says More, was the dualism of classical philosophy mingled with Christian theology: reason and impulse in the natural order, supernatural insight above them. But the age so wasted itself in religious wars that all religion fell into disrepute and an age of naturalism followed. The dominant philosophy of the eighteenth century was a rationalism that denied the existence of supernatural revelation and looked to reason alone for authority. But men have instincts and emotions as well as reason, and there soon arose a revolt against reason on behalf of these forces. When the nineteenth century opened, the world stood divided between the followers of rationalism and romanticism. Now, the most dangerous error of romanticism is not its anti-rationalism, but the illusion that it is a return to spiritual insight. Romanticism would substitute the limitless expansiveness of our impulsive nature for the true infinite in man which is above both reason and emotion and which is felt as restraint, centrality, form. Hence its compatibility with science. The limitless forces of nature which hypothetical or metaphysical science has raised into a self-evolving universe are the exact counterpart of the limitless desires of the heart, and the two are united in that very modern philosophy which we indifferently term romantic or scientific.

V *Humanitarian Literature*

Of all the vast literature which toward the end of the nineteenth century undertook to study the social position of the Church in the contemporary world, one of the oddest forms was the popular social-gospel novel.[8] By and large sentimental and optimistic, it based its appeal on religious idealism, sympathy for the oppressed, the novelty of its economic and social proposals, and the doctrine of Christian stewardship. Beginning in 1883 with Washington Gladden's *The Christian League of Connecticut* and continuing down through the end of the century, the social-gospel novel developed in a variety of forms the theme of the obligation of the Church toward the establishment of an industrial democracy, a cooperative commonwealth, or even Christian Socialism. Some of its titles are suggestive of its tenor: Albion W. Tourgée's *Murvale Eastman, Christian Socialist;* William T. Stead's *If Christ Came to Chicago;* Edward Everett Hale's *If Jesus Came to Boston;* an anonymous *Christ the Socialist;* Charles M. Sheldon's *In His Steps, or What Would Jesus Do?* which, after the Bible and Mickey Spillane, is possibly the greatest seller of all time and which Sheldon followed with *In His Steps Today;* Florence Converse's *The Burden of Christopher,* and James L. Smiley's *Maud Miller's Ministry, or the Claims of Christian Socialism.*

This abundance of humanitarian religious fiction was part of a larger body of fiction on social and economic problems. From 1861, when the *Atlantic* published Rebecca Harding Davis's "Life in the Iron Mills," economic fiction appeared with increasing frequency; it is prominent in the works of such writers as Hamlin Garland, William Dean Howells, and Frank Norris. Some of it was conservative in its leanings and some liberal, but all of it was middle class and respectable. Conservative works emphasized the virtues of old-fashioned American individualism and the dangers of organized labor; liberal works advocated moderate reforms and complained of stock jobbery, the oppression of small business by big, the corruption of legislatures, the evils of the mortgage system, the monotony and demoralization of labor, and other evils. Liberal solutions were often economic— the organization of labor, for instance—but often simply moral, with the aim of awakening the humanitarianism of the upper classes and extending the feeling of brotherly love.

Florence Converse's *The Burden of Christopher,* which like many another work of the times was both a social-gospel and an economic novel, is the story of Christopher Kenyon, whose humane policies in the operation of his shoe mill—profit-sharing, eight-hour day, union wages, and the like—run him so deeply into debt that he embezzles some money from a widow with seven children. Even this remedy fails him, and with the statement, "There was nobody else even willing to sin for the men,"[9] he kills himself. In 1914 More referred to *The Burden of Christopher* as "the first popular presentation" to come to his attention of the new morality of humanitarianism, but he had first mentioned it in *The Jessica Letters* (67-68) of 1904, by which time he was well acquainted with humanitarian literature. Since Wordsworth, he believed, there had grown up a tradition of writers for whom art is an attempt to enoble the common and bring the proud into sympathy with the vulgar. While this tradition has enlisted few writers of the first importance, it is strong in popular literature—More cites the reputations of Mary Wilkins Freeman and Edwin Markham as evidence—and it accounts for the general decline of literature in our day. The themes which have made the great literature of the West are those of personal honor and responsibility to God, rather than any mawkish sentimentality. The great dramatists and poets see that the individual life is made significant by being brought into relation with some general law or communal interest. Such modern writers as Tolstoy, Ibsen, Hauptmann, Gorky, and Zola are in this tradition, except that they have lost the sense of man's community in the moral or spiritual world and have found it instead in his lower nature. Literature is the child of its age, and its present amorality is the result of a wider revolution than a literary one. We have given up interest in personal morality for a vaguer social consciousness.[10]

After 1900 the economic novel became more radical in tone, increasingly advocating fundamental changes in the economic system; its fortunes, in fact, rose and fell with those of the Socialist Party. Among the early radical novels the best known today are Upton Sinclair's *The Jungle* (1906), Jack London's *The Iron Heel* (1908), and Ernest Poole's *The Harbor* (1915). As literary editor of the *Independent,* the *Nation,* and the New York *Evening Post* and as reviewer for these and other periodicals, More must have seen dozens of such books, but he wrote about only a few. *The Harbor,* which Walter B. Rideout calls "the best Socialist novel of them all" (56), was one of these.

More is interested in *The Harbor,* as in *The Burden of Christopher,* for the same reason that he is interested in Jane Addams and John Dewey. Toward the end of the novel someone says, ". . . a man if he's to be vital at all must give up the idea of any fixed creed. . . . But if he does, if he holds himself open to change and knows change in his very life, then he can get a serenity which is as much better than that of the monk as living is better than dying."[11] More dismisses the novel as a literary work, preferring to discuss it as sociology. Its hero sees the emptiness of a world run by scientific efficiency but devoid of human values, and his remedy for its wars and its oppression is sympathy. But what is his sympathy and the sympathy of all such reformers, asks More, but fear? The proletariat have united out of fear of oppression and now threaten their oppressors; the upper classes, sensing their doom, have been driven to "a morality of sympathy and sops in place of obligation and command" (*SE,* XI, 251). It may be true, More concedes, that fear is inevitable in human life; but if it is, history shows that fear of God is more potent for human happiness than fear of any other kind. Fear of God holds the individual responsible for his actions, and if a sense of responsibility were once again instilled into society, men might find it easier to use scientific efficiency for their good.

VI *Conservatism*

One of the marks of More's criticism of social, economic, and political issues is its philosophical quality, its concern with principle. He occasionally names persons who are prominent in the various movements he opposes and occasionally cites instances of the mischief of reform, but in general his essays have a theoretical tone, the persons and instances he mentions being only particular manifestations of the larger moral evils that are his real concern. There are two explanations for this trait. One is that while granting economics and politics their own laws, More views them also as social extensions of ethics, and their moral aspects are what interest him. The second is his belief that, being essentially moral, they can be best understood in the light of unchanging moral laws which have been effectively propounded by philosophers and statesmen over the centuries. It is therefore sometimes difficult to relate the political thought of his essays to the political environment which provoked them, although his letters, naturally, are more specific.

In both More's letters and essays Theodore Roosevelt appears as an incarnation of the sentimental aspirations of humanitarian democracy. In "Natural Aristocracy" he is, without being named, the very model of a demagogue, persuading the people that their current impulse is their safest guide and that they should destroy those institutions which they have erected in wiser moments as safeguards against impulsive action (SE, IX, 22-27). More was justified in taking Roosevelt as the embodiment of reform, and perhaps right also in distrusting him; many of the reformers themselves, like LaFollette, suspected him of opportunism and charlatanry. Although Roosevelt began his administration by opposing the prohibition of trusts, as his first term wore on he secured more and more legislation for the regulation of business and the protection of labor; his second election encouraged him to further reforms. Many conservatives thought him too radical and many radicals too conservative, but he ended his second term at the peak of his popularity. More had begun to fear that "that explosive nuisance of the White House" would seek another term.[12]

Roosevelt, however, not only did not run, he surprised the country by selecting the conservative Taft as his successor. Despite the Rooseveltian tenor of the party platform, Taft, once elected, began to conciliate the Republicans whom Roosevelt had offended and to alienate the progressives in the party. A number of reform measures were passed during his administration; but largely through fights over tariffs, conservation, and congressional rules changes he steadily repelled the progressives, who began

thinking of LaFollette for their nominee in 1912. In February
of that year, during an illness of LaFollette's, Roosevelt announced his candidacy. The campaign between Roosevelt and
Taft was personal and sharp, Taft warning of Roosevelt's in-
consistenceis and emotionalism, Roosevelt complaining of in-
gratitude. More thought Taft had made a mistake in being drawn
into a quarrel by the "blackguardism" of that "demon of malign
energy."[13] When Roosevelt split the party after the Republicans
renominated Taft, Woodrow Wilson won the election.

The change had little effect on More's view of the trend in
American politics, for he came to detest Wilson more than he did
any other politician, "even Bryan." More thought that a good
essay might be written "on the effects of humanitarianism as
we see it working in Wilson,"[14] but he never wrote it, and we
have only his general views on humanitarianism and some scattered comments on Wilson from which to piece out his opinion
and the reasons behind it. That Wilson stood for humanitarian
reform would be enough of an explanation, but some of Wilson's
own actions also disturbed More. He believed that after the
election of 1916 Wilson had set about deliberately to arouse
German hostility in order to advance his political interests,[15]
and that toward the end of the war he rejected the Germans'
first overtures toward peace because, demagogically, he sensed
that the mood of the country was against them. Wrote More: "I
do detest and distrust the man."[16]

In 1915 More collected "Natural Aristocracy" and a number
of other essays he had been publishing over the preceding two
years in *Aristocracy and Justice.* His purpose is to oppose the
social implications of evolution with the conservative wisdom
of literature and philosophy. In two ways the book is the culmination of his political thought. First, More describes in
"Natural Aristocracy" and "Academic Leadership" the kind of
leadership the conservatives need and how to go about obtain-
ing it; second, in "Justice," "Property and Law," and "Disraeli
and Conservatism," he discusses the principles of conservatism.
"The Socialism of G. Lowes Dickinson," published five years
earlier in another volume (*SE,* VII, 170-94), would have fitted
nicely into *Aristocracy and Justice,* since it also touches on
those subjects.

Our problem today, runs the argument of *Aristocracy and
Justice,* is one of leadership. How can a democratic society be

persuaded to be guided by an aristocracy which has none of the traditional aristocratic resources for imposing its power? Demagogues maintain that the cure for the evils of democracy is more democracy, but the claim is false and they know it. What democracy really needs is some means of recognizing the natural aristocracy which can be found in any wholesome society and of conferring power upon it, and the first step toward satisfying this need is that the men who form that aristocracy should come to an understanding of their own power and responsibilities. The power of the masses is an exaggerated evil; the real danger to any society is the corruption or submission of its natural leaders. A class consciousness among this group, through which they could assure one another of their mutual support and strengthen the hesitant among them, would be the best safeguard against such a danger.

Popular government, however, depends inevitably on the molding of public opinion; and public opinion is most effectively controlled through the power of the imagination, by which More means that it is not rational appeal which wins popular support but those means which capture the faith and arouse the emotions of a people—pageant, ritual, history, and tradition. Formerly, the union that existed between aristocracy and hereditary oligarchy provided a visible and definite source of imaginative appeal; lacking that advantage, modern societies must find some other way of strengthening the vaguer aristocracy of character. The best means to this end are the colleges and universities, for if these institutions can be recalled from their current interest in such studies as economics and sociology—an interest which isolates the student from the past and "debauches his mind with a flabby, or inflames it with a fanatic, humanitarianism" (37)—and if they can be made instead to restore to prominence those courses which train the imagination and instill a sense of history, they can strengthen the men they educate with the equivalent of the knowledge and self-confidence which came to hereditary oligarchy by prescription.

In other words, since what is needed is an aristocracy of intellect and character, the problem of leadership is a problem of education: What course of study best serves the needs of a natural aristocracy? More's answer is the classics, because they surpass all rival studies—all modern languages and literature and all the sciences, though mathematics and physics belong in any education—in the discipline they require of their students and because better than any other studies they impart to their students a common range of ideas and a single point of view. He is not for curtailing scholarly work in any specialized branch of study; he merely insists that educated men should have a common body of humane knowledge. But in addition to inculcating an aristocracy of intellect, the classics would ally the natural aristocracy of the present with the aristocracies of the past. It is in Homer, Pindar, and Aeschylus, in Plato, Aristotle, and Cicero that the aristocratic ideal appears in its purest form, and the classical and humanist tradition has been the mainstay of Anglo-Saxon aristocracy from the beginning.[17]

The very idea of an aristocracy, More admits, will seem harsh and unjust to all reformers, who judge all things by their feelings; yet the idea, despite apparent similarities, is not the same as Nietzsche's more brutal though apparently more rational conception. Unlike humanitarianism, Nietzscheism, or any other social theory derived from an evolutionary conception of nature, the idea of a true aristocracy rests on a right understanding of justice. Justice demands that power and privilege, and "property as the symbol and instrument of these" (120), be given to superior men, though insofar as possible without the suffering or the oppression of the weak. Although governments will always find it difficult to meet this ideal, they must nonetheless aim at it, for it is the only view of society compatible with the realities of human nature. Human nature, not property, is the cause of greed and injustice. Simple redistribution of property, then, would not make men happy, though it could destroy civilization as we know it. Mere life is a pretty primitive thing, and all that makes it worthwhile, from the simplest material necessity to the highest production of art, is associated with property. Therefore —and this conclusion of More's has infuriated more people than any other he ever expressed—"to the civilized man *the rights of property are more important than the right to life*" (136).

Men do not legislate, More contends; they only discover those laws of nature and morality which God has given. From this it follows that human laws can never be regarded as codes of virtue which, once they are realized, can cure society of its ills; they are only sets of practical regulations governing society for limited ends. Ignorant of this fact and relying merely on theory, the humanitarians would adapt the institutions of government to man as he ought to be rather than as he is. Just and reasonable men, on the other hand, must uphold the rigor of the law, which for the larger good of society and despite its inequalities is primarily concerned with the rights of property.

But such a view is not an acceptance of materialism. The greatest encouragement of materialism, in fact, is the very unsettling of property to which the humanitarians contribute. It is for this reason that the Church and the university have always been conservative, for they know that *"if property is secure, it may be the means to an end, whereas if it is insecure it will be the end itself"* (148). The conservative, however, sees as well as the liberal the inevitability and even the good of change. He differs from the liberal in denying that all change is progress and in tolerating only those changes which correct specific abuses without subverting social order. Liberalism believes in the essential goodness of human nature and the rightness of its impulses toward change; conservatism rests "on a certain distrust of human nature" and "in the controlling power of imagination" (168).

More's statement that the Church and the university have always been conservative is, whatever its historical validity, a reflection of his belief that true religion and an imaginative understanding of history are incompatible with socialism. Socialism does appeal, More admits, to men of religion and imagination, but only to those whose religion and imagination are somehow defective or to those who are not both religious and imaginative at the same time. Those "who really cherish literature and the arts" commonly distrust it (*SE*, VII, 179-80). When men of imagination are drawn to it, More believes, the reason is that they find nothing in an economic and utilitarian society which can hold their allegiance. They might console themselves with religion, looking to a future state for the recompense of present wrongs; but too frequently their belief in religion has been undermined by modern science and philosophy, and they find their Supreme Good in the love of man for man, thus falling victim "to the dominant party of discontent" (*SE*, VII, 193-94).

In the same way, men who have a religious inclination but no imaginative grasp of tradition to support it tend to find their future consolation in temporal affairs. The surest sign of a lessening of faith is a turning from imaginative possession of the past, which being now beyond the possibility of change stands as a symbol of the eternal, to that "hankering after a future which is no more than a glorification, as it is a desired product, of change itself" (*SE*, VII, 133-34). Because of this intimate connection between imagination and leadership, More believes, it is very important to the culture of a nation that its artists, the custodians of its imagination, be allied with its power. England fell from the intellectual leadership of Europe during the eighteenth century because after 1714 her imagination and her practical sense became alienated from each other (*SE*, X, 135-36).

VII *Critique of More's Conservatism*

More could not have hoped to convert his opponents by the essays of *Aristocracy and Justice*. He seems rather to have wanted to make, for the benefit of anyone who shared his beliefs, an uncompromising statement of the principles of conservatism. Fellow conservatives believe that he did;[18] many of his opponents confuse him with what he opposed. Van Wyck Brooks, for example, incensed over the statement that *"the rights of property are more important than the right to life,"* denounced him for his "faith in a society based . . . upon the acquisitive instincts of man, a society ruled over by the 'natural aristocracy' of economic power."[19] The charge is simply untrue. More's faith in an aristocracy was not based on any illusion that the individual aristocrat was innately superior to the common man or on any naive identification of economic power with character. It came from a conviction that—by some process which, however paradoxical, could be seen at work in history—selfish men, inspired by selfish motives, produced virtually in spite of themselves and only as a by-product of their immediate objectives something far better than what they aimed at, and that this better thing, becoming institutionalized, took on a life of its own and in its turn raised the general level of society.

> The aristocratic theory presupposes that the ideal of a family set apart by a certain illusion, if you please, of the people for the higher ends of life will, imperfectly no doubt, work itself out in a practice of honour and beauty and wise control on the part of the family itself, and in a maintenance in society at large of values which have no relation to production. It believes that the concealment of labour in an inherited name may have this power of imagination, and that in the long run and in general

the artificial distinction of rank has fostered the true distinction of character. It hopes that, as the aristocracy of artificial distinctions passes away, there may arise an aristocracy of true distinctions. (*SE*, VII, 179)

As early as 1901 in an anonymous editorial, "The Gospel of Wealth,"[20] More pointed to the evil effects on public morality of the preachments and example of Charles W. Schwab, John D. Rockefeller, and Andrew Carnegie: "they are pernicious, they are a public offense, an humiliation to the country." The following year, in "Wealth and Culture,"[21] he ascribed the lack of any native American culture worthy of the name to the fact that the national ideal, an ideal of "material wealth and its complement of socialism or humanitarianism," was incapable of sustaining one. And in 1904 he concluded *The Jessica Letters* with the complaint that men alternate "between the sickly sympathies of Hull House and the sordid cruelties of Wall Street" (299) because they have no vision beyond the material. He believed that the reformers merely wanted to give the poor what the rich now had, that their appeals to religion disguised a purely material concern, and that without attacking the real source of social discontent they were likely to do infinite damage.

There is some truth in all these contentions. Except for the "merely," many reformers would admit to the first; some, as More knew, never appealed to religion. By its very nature the third can hardly be answered. Most modern liberals would agree with More that the ultimate cause of social discontent can never be removed, but they could not accept his estimate of the risks of reform. More's charges are a variation of that old polemical claim that the enemy is either a knave or a fool, and they are made further suspect because they come from a man who seems at times almost pathologically opposed to any contemporary thought or impulse. Yet, whatever the temperamental origins of More's conservatism, his position was also a matter of reason and conviction, and it was never smug or complacent. He was "not afraid of being called a reactionary," he once admitted, "if only the word is properly taken."[22] But he also admitted that it was "a desperately hard thing to go all one's life against the current of one's age."[23]

The difference between Paul Elmer More and the social Darwinists with whom his critics—Van Wyck Brooks, for ex-

ample—often lump him is the difference between traditional
and Darwinian conservatism which Richard Hofstadter describes
in *Social Darwinism in American Thought.* Social Darwinism was
entirely secular, held no reverence for traditional authority, and
substituted for those "sentimental and emotional ties" which
More called "imaginative" a rationalistic conception of social
relationships. Hofstadter illustrates his distinction with a contrast
between Edmund Burke, who typifies traditional conservatism,
and William Graham Sumner, one of the most prominent spokesmen of social Darwinism at the turn of the century in America.
Whereas Burke was a religious man who relied on an intuitive approach to politics and on instinctive wisdom, Sumner was a
thoroughgoing secularist and rationalist. Burke relied on a collective, long-range intelligence, on the wisdom of the community
at large; for Sumner, wisdom spoke through individual self-asser-
tion. Burke revered custom, historical continuity, the past; Sumner regarded reverence for the old order as sentimentalism (7-8).
What Hofstadter says of Burke is without exception true of More.

Hofstadter also says that "Burke's conservatism seems relatively
timeless and placeless, while Sumner's seems to belong pre-
eminently to the post-Darwinian era and to America" (8).
Here too More resembles Burke, but the "timeless," "placeless,"
and un-American qualities of his conservatism are a weakness
as well as a strength. He too often seems remote from the
concrete situations with which his essays deal, as I have already
said, and his conservatism is somewhat lacking in the vividness
and imaginative appeal which by his own standards it should
have. Even his language reflects the defect, as when he somewhat grandiloquently describes the true aim of the state as "to
make possible the high friendship of those who have raised
themselves to a vision of the supreme good" (*SE*, IX, 35). Aristotle's state perhaps, but ours? In the same way, his reliance on
the colleges and universities, it seems to me, reflects a miscon-
ception of the prestige of these institutions in America and of the
historical tendencies of American higher education. It might have
been possible in 1915 to hope for a revival of the classics; except
for service courses in "communications," there is some doubt
today about English. Nor have the universities ever held in
America the positions which Oxford and Cambridge might once
have held in England. Such opinions, as he says of the reformers'
conceptions of government, have too much a hypothetical air.

More seems, in other words, to have insufficiently distinguished between the British and the American traditions in politics and in society. A strong Anglophile all his life, he was charmed by British speech;[24] and when he collected his essays into books to be read on both sides of the Atlantic, he had them revised to follow British forms in spelling. It was a visit to England that inspired the meditations of *Pages from an Oxford Diary,* and he came to look upon Anglicanism as the nearest possibility to a completely satisfactory religion.[25] In his last illness he wondered whether life might not have been richer for him had he gone in 1914 to England rather than to Princeton.[26] Yet he was not for all this any less a patriot. When it began to appear that he was likely to be better appreciated in England than in America, he was saddened by the prospect, "for after all *Americanus Sum.*"[27]

His fusion of the British and the American traditions and the consequent weakness of his argument, however, are most apparent not in his passing remarks on the conservatism of the universities and the Church, but in his description of the conservative tradition in politics and in the names of his great conservatives. In neither of these does an American appear. And naturally, for there has been no influential conservative tradition in America, in More's sense of the term, since the end of the eighteenth century. Richard Hofstadter finds his best example of traditional conservatism in Burke, even though his book deals with American history. In *The Conservative Mind,* which is devoted, like More's *Aristocracy and Justice,* to encouraging conservatism, Russell Kirk shows that political conservatism is more British than American. More recently, Clinton Rossiter, in *Conservatism in America,*[28] has demonstrated the same conclusion. While insisting that there is a strong conservative element in American history, Rossiter must nevertheless admit that "the American political tradition is basically a Liberal tradition" (68), and his survey of American history from 1607 to 1933 shows that, in the sense in which More used the word, conservatism has scarcely existed in the United States since the days of Washington and John Adams. It is understandable that the names More invokes in *Aristocracy and Justice* are the names of Burke, Disraeli, and Plato. Except for John C. Calhoun and Orestes Brownson (a conservative in his later life), whom else was he to name?

CHAPTER 4

Platonism and Christianity

I *The Greek Tradition*

AFTER RESIGNING from the *Nation* early in 1914 to devote himself to independent scholarship, More was soon at work on a critical and historical study of Platonism which would run to six volumes covering the eight and a half centuries from the death of Socrates in 399 B.C. to the Council of Chalcedon in A.D. 451. *Platonism* appeared in 1917, but it was not at first part of any larger work, and *The Greek Tradition* proper begins with *The Religion of Plato* in 1921. *Hellenistic Philosophies* appeared in 1923, *The Christ of the New Testament* in 1924, and *Christ the Word* in 1927. *Platonism*, which had been listed in *Hellenistic Philosophies* as an Introductory Volume to *The Greek Tradition*, was formally incorporated into the series in a revised, second edition of 1926—although the revisions are not substantial—and is referred to in later lists of the series as a Complementary Volume along with *The Catholic Faith*, published in 1931, the last volume in the series. *The Sceptical Approach to Religion*, published in 1934 as the second volume of *New Shelburne Essays*, covered much the same material, but from a different point of view.[1]

Taken in order of appearance, these titles indicate a shift in emphasis from philosophical speculation to Christian doctrine; in this they reflect a change that occurred in More's own values during the time of his writing. When he began *Platonism* he held to the religious conceptions we find in the *Shelburne Essays* —to the belief that there is a "truth which is in religion but is not bounded by religious dogma, and which needs no confirmation by miracle or inspired tradition" (*P*, vii-viii). By the time he had finished *The Christ of the New Testament*, he was convinced that for himself at least, religious certainty depended on divine revelation. The volumes followed, however, the general aim he defined in *Platonism*: "to lay the foundation for a series of studies on the origins and early environment of Christianity and on such more modern movements as the English revival of philosophical religion in the seventeenth century and the rise of romanticism in the eighteenth" (*P*, v).

As More describes it, the Greek tradition began with the pre-philosophical teachings of Socrates. These were developed by his disciples into a number of philosophical schools of which only Platonism was a true development of the teachings of the master, all the others being rationalizations of some one aspect of the Socratic doctrine. So great was the confusion produced by the contentions among these various schools that in the Hellenistic era Greek philosophy virtually collapsed and might have disappeared altogether had it not been revived by the introduction into the West of the Christian doctrine of the Incarnation, which merged with Platonism in the gospel of St. John to the advantage of both Platonism and Christianity. Immediately, however, the Church was divided by theological disputes among the rationalizers of various aspects of the doctrine of the Incarnation—just as Hellenistic philosophy had been divided—until first at the Council of Nicea and then at the Council of Chalcedon the Church affirmed, in the simplest language consistent with full expression of the truth, the one essential doctrine of Christianity, which is also a confirmation of the teachings of Socrates and Plato.

The Greek tradition is therefore cyclical and progressive: a pagan phase is followed by a Christian phase which is built upon the pagan and takes the same pattern. Each phase begins with the discovery or assertion of a truth; there is then a development of the truth to the furthest point of understanding and consistency, then a corruption of the truth, and then a simple reassertion of it—the reassertion that comes at the end of the pagan phase being, of course, the initial point of the Christian. Platonism is thus the philosophical preparation of Christianity, and Christianity is the culmination of Platonism. More sees no special significance, however, in the correspondences between the pagan and the Christian halves of the tradition other than that they show how the mind is faced with the unavoidable alternatives of "a reasonable philosophy based on an irrational paradox" and "an unreasonable metaphysic based on a rational presumption" (*CW*, 137). The tradition might also be described in the figure of converging streams, since the line of Messianic prophecy which was the preparation for the Incarnation and which More discusses in *The Christ of the New Testament* meets the dualism of Plato only after each has had an independent development. More is describing the Greek tradition, however, and not the Judaeo-Christian one; and we may point out without impugning either the sincerity or the intensity of his religious devotion, both of which are evident in the series, that he is less interested in Plato because Plato confirms Christ than he is interested in Christ because Christ confirms the dualism of Plato and Socrates and, beyond that, the dualism of More's own experience.

II *Platonism*

The argument of *Platonism* is that the teachings of Socrates consist of three principal elements: intellectual skepticism, an affirmation of the reality of the spiritual life and of the difference between good and evil, and a belief in the identity of virtue and knowledge. These teachings were "the determining event in the moral and religious life of the Western world; for the supreme need of man's soul is not that he should acquire a splendid system of philosophy, but that he should hold as an inexpugnable possession that spirit of scepticism and insight and that assurance of the identity of virtue and knowledge for which Socrates lived and died" (*P*, 13-14). But while these elements are the core of philosophy, they are not philosophy in themselves. Socrates merely affirmed the common belief that virtue leads to happiness and vice to pain, and he defended it with an ironic skepticism and the myth of a supernatural judgment. It remained for Plato, in his own speculations in the later *Dialogues,* to make the teachings of Socrates into a true philosophy by subjecting them to rational analysis.

The Socrates of the *Protagoras* made virtue a hedonistic science based on the pleasure and pain which follow human actions: when a man errs, he does so because he does not accurately foresee the true pleasurable or painful consequences of what he is doing. But in the *Gorgias,* a later dialogue in which Plato presents his own doctrine, Socrates distinguishes between good and bad pleasures and thus undercuts a purely hedonistic ethic. The conclusions of *The Republic* are based upon the same dualism—upon the distinction, that is, between lower and higher pleasures, between pleasure and true happiness. Happiness is a state of tranquillity which arises within the soul of the man who is master of himself, who inhibits the workings of his impulsive nature; it is both the consequence and the measure of his justice. Our knowledge of justice, therefore, is not a matter of sense perception but of intuition. We live in a phenomenal world and have knowledge of it; this lower knowledge is what Plato calls opinion. Above it is another kind, fixed, certain, and unaffected by the flux of perceptual experience; this is the only true knowledge.

From the knowledge that we are happy when we act after due exercise of our inhibiting will and miserable when we do not, we derive our sense of responsibility for our actions; from this sense, in turn, comes our awareness of the freedom of the will. But since freedom of the will "can exist only by virtue of an inhibitive power of the soul, the so-called will to refrain, entirely distinct from the positive will which is determined by the final predominance of one impulse over another," we are thrown back "upon a radical psychological dualism and upon a cosmic dualism of good and evil as its counterpart" (P, 150)—upon a dualism of good and evil, that is, which is not merely psychological but subsists in the very universe we inhabit. Like all theologians, Plato fell at times into the metaphysical error of trying to reconcile evil with the goodness of God; admitting finally that the coexistence of good and evil was ultimately inexplicable, he gave his view of it in the form of a myth. His abandonment of metaphysical reasoning is an admission of his inability to achieve something no philosopher has ever achieved or ever will, since the problem lies beyond the comprehension of human reason.

Owing to inconsistencies in Plato's own thought, More admits, there is some confusion about the Platonic ideas. The difficulties, however, are chiefly with the rational ideas, those that are mathematical or otherwise quantitative, rather than with the ethical, in which Plato's principal interest lay. These ethical ideas, an assertion of the objectivity and changelessness of the moral law, are not a product of the metaphysical reason, but of the imagination properly employed. Just as the imagination projects new combinations of sense impressions into a kind of existence outside the mind, it constructs out of its moral experiences a positive representation of the virtues and projects this too into an autonomous existence which the soul then seems to reach out to possess. These projections are the Platonic ideas; the manner of their construction explains their nebulous quality. Though we are certain of their existence, they melt away the moment we consider them with the discursive reason or try to describe them in terms satisfactory to reason.

Nevertheless, we have pragmatic evidence of their objectivity. Men who admit the reality of the idea of justice, say, will love justice and, their love directed to something fixed and imaginatively impressive, will be more concerned than otherwise to establish it in their souls. Those who deny it and with it anything more permanent than the transiencies of custom take away all that gives justice a firm hold upon men. Without the objective reality of the ideas, there is no sound basis for morality; the ideas are the very foundation of the spiritual life.

Through knowledge of the ideas the soul passes upward to the notion of God. When man inhibits some desire, he performs an act of temperance from which he derives a feeling of happiness. The repetition of such events gives him a larger experience of happiness and of virtue and makes temperance more attractive to him. As he reflects upon his experience, the idea of temperance expands, first perhaps into the idea of fortitude, the virtue of resisting all temptation, then into something larger yet, and finally into the supreme idea of the good. Although the good is impossible to define, once we come upon it and gain familiarity with it, we begin to see it in its other aspects. As it exists in the material world and in the characters of men we call it beauty, and through contemplation of beauty we pass to the supreme idea of beauty. To do so is not to surrender the soul to physical allurements; it is rather to reject such allurements even while appreciating them and to discover something akin to the inner check manifesting itself in the world and drawing the soul, by the allurements of the world, from the world and to itself. With this experience we discover God, and philosophy passes into religion.

More describes religion in *The Religion of Plato* as "an emotion, an aspiration, a faith, a knowledge, a life, a something" (*RP*, 278) produced by the mingling and cooperation of philosophy, theology, and mythology. Philosophy consists of those conclusions which men reach, through their reason and immediate experience alone, concerning their nature and their place in the universe; it is "the soul's discovery of itself, as an entity having a law and interests of its own apart from and above all this mixed and incomprehensible life of the body" (*RP*, 48). Theology, more speculative and therefore less firmly grounded in certain knowledge, is the study of God and of man's relation to Him. Even further removed from the facts of experience, although still rooted in them, mythology is the allegorical or imaginative rendering of sublime truths, the dramatization of the discoveries of philosophy and theology. Taken by itself or magnified out of due proportion, any one of the three elements tends to corruption. Philosophy may become so austere and impersonal as to lose its appeal to the human soul; theology leads to fanaticism; mythology degenerates into superstition. Yet philosophy should be the dominant element in any religion, for its certainties are the beginnings of theological conjecture and the means of judging and limiting mythology.

The differences between Platonism and Christianity are the results of their originating, respectively, in philosophy and in mythology. Plato begins with philosophy and considers theology and mythology as appendages, however necessary, to the central truth. The Christian begins with mythology—without the Incarnation, his faith is meaningless—and regards philosophy and theology as the gropings of a ruined intelligence. For the Christian, only belief in a judgment to come assures justice in this life; for the Platonist, the soul of man is a stronger guarantor of justice than any external constraint. Nevertheless, Plato does believe in the existence of God, in divine providence, and in the inexorability of divine justice. The qualities of his God are immutability, goodness or beneficence, and wisdom; but "omniscience, omnipotence, ubiquity, and other metaphysical abstractions . . . are repudiated by the whole tenor of his theology and mythology" (*RP*, 119). Plato's God, therefore, does not resemble the cold abstraction of metaphysics; but neither has He the definiteness, vividness, and personality of the God of the Christians and Jews. Yet He has all the attributes necessary for true religion.

With *Hellenistic Philosophies* More pauses in his discussion of Platonism to take up a number of rival philosophies, and he does not return to the central Platonic tradition until *Christ the Word,* except for some brief remarks in *The Christ of the New*

Testament on the Platonism of St. John's gospel. The philosophical schools which he examines in *Hellenistic Philosophies*—Epicureanism, Stoicism, Neoplatonism, and Skepticism or Pyrrhonism—have their origins directly or indirectly in Socrates, but they differ both from the philosophy of Plato and from one another in that each is a rationalization or disproportionate emphasis of one of the three elements of the teachings of Socrates. The Epicureans and the Stoics rationalized the identification of virtue and knowledge, although some of the Stoics were ambiguous; the Neoplatonists rationalized the spiritual affirmation; the Pyrrhonists accepted the skepticism and rejected the other two elements.

There is no need to discuss More's treatment of all these schools or of the individual philosophers he singles out for special treatment. His discussion of Plotinus, however, is of particular interest in view of Plotinus' claim to having restored the teaching of Plato and in view of the place of religious mysticism in Neoplatonism, to which More will give attention in *The Catholic Faith*. More does not, by the way, give any detailed treatment to the history of true Platonism after Plato, an omission which is somewhat unfortunate. The claim he later makes in *Christ the Word*, that Christianity, which merged with Platonism in the fourth century, is the logical culmination of Platonism, would be stronger—at least clearer—if he were to show the continuity of the Platonic tradition in itself.

Neoplatonism, in More's opinion, is a perversion of Platonism —something close enough to the original in its philosophy and mythology, in its analysis of the actual experience of men and in its projection of that experience into cosmic forces, but quite un-Platonic in undertaking a rational explanation of the causes of things. More suspects that Neoplatonism is a combination of the Aristotelian Unmoved Mover and the idea, taken from various Oriental religions, of a creating God who dwells beyond the realm of movement and change. Whatever its origins, Neoplatonism is a double corruption of Platonism. First, it interprets Plato as believing that ideas exist only in the mind and are not objective to it; and, in so doing, Neoplatonism deprives philosophy of objective authority. Second, in the importance it attaches to mysticism, it identifies religious experience with emotional excess, thereby offering as compensation for our ignorance of God the illusion of union with Him.

Interesting also, because of More's claim that the Platonist is the only true skeptic, is his discussion of Skepticism and Pyrrhonism, which he considers a single phenomenon. Unable to choose between the various Hellenistic philosophies, the Skeptic took refuge in suspension of judgment; from Pyrrho to Sextus Empiricus—from 270 B.C. to A.D. 230—the basic contention of the Skeptics was that man had no certain knowledge of the truth. In a sense the Skeptic gained some measure of liberty and security, the goals of all philosophy. He chose the pleasures life offered without involving himself in insoluble questions about their ultimate causes; while he denied the existence of moral law, he relied in practical affairs on custom and common sense. But his position, though understandable as a reaction to the situation of Hellenistic philosophy, is the denial of philosophy. And it is not true skepticism.

True knowledge, for the skeptic of whatever variety, consists only of those immediate affections about which there can be no doubt. Of these there are two kinds, material and spiritual. The Pyrrhonist may not explicitly deny the spiritual, but in basing his life on the material alone he virtually denies it. The Platonist, on the other hand, lives his life in the full range of the affections. Because their experience of the spirit is less insistent than their experience of matter and because reason, always in rebellion against dualism, lends its authority to matter, men frequently conclude that the spirit is illusion. Resisting this alliance of reason and desire and affirming the reality of the spirit, the Platonist is the only true skeptic, insisting on the truth of what consciousness tells him even if he cannot define it to the satisfaction of reason.

As the Hellenistic world drew to a close, men were ready for something new in morality and belief—for some stronger authority than the discredited philosophies of the period. Epicureanism and Stoicism held no attraction for the mass of the people; in any event, they offered no sure guide in conduct or belief. Neoplatonism had become encrusted with magic and superstition. But in theology and mythology, the only authorities to rival philosophy, we have not certainty but only varying degrees of probability. If there is any escape in religion from the limitation of probability, it does not come through the use of unassisted reason, "but must wait on a revelation which comes with its own authority of immediate conviction." Such a revelation the Christian finds "in the life and words of the historic Jesus" (*HP*, 370).

III *Platonism and the Early Church*

Originally intending to treat the development of Christianity down to the year 451 in a single volume in which the New Testament would provide only "an episode," More required two volumes for the task (*CNT*, vii). *The Christ of the New Testament* considers the Hebrew tradition of the Messiah and how Jesus fitted into it, the life and death of Jesus, His preachings and their relations both to the Jewish law and to what we know of human morality from other sources, the interpretations of Jesus which are presented in the gospels and in St. Paul, and the validity of His claims to be the Son of God. *Christ the Word* deals with the religious beliefs of the early Church; the first major assaults on the true faith from the Gnostics without and from the Sabellians, Arians, Nestorians, and Monophysites within; the Council of Nicea in 325 and the Council of Chalcedon in 451; the relationship of the dogmas of these Councils to the tradition of Greek philosophy; and the significance of the doctrine of the Logos both in the early Church and for us. Their combined purpose is to show that the doctrine of the Incarnation, with its union of the human and the divine, is the one essential doctrine of Christianity and the culminating expression of an idea which began in the dualism of Plato.

The Christ of the New Testament is partly historical reconstruction of the life and personality of Jesus—and in this More acknowledges his indebtedness to the higher criticism, even protesting his intention of saving it from its ideological assumptions—and partly interpretation and argument. There are also two attitudes More displays toward his material—that of the objective student and that of the reverent believer. Where the historical record is faulty, he tries to reconstruct it; but he goes only so far in his attempt, finding as he approaches the events of Christ's passion and death that the mystery is more than he cares to meddle with:

> I have had no intention to retell these last events of Jesus' life, least of all to offer any obtrusive comments on the agony in the garden of Gesthemane, and the consummation on Calvary. As often as I have read these chapters in all my years from early childhood, I cannot now approach them without being moved to the innermost. Here humanity touches the lowest depths and the

highest exaltation. Who was he that in the hour of death forgot the desertion of his disciples, forgot his hopes and transient victories, but not his divine claims: "My God, why hast thou forsaken me!" He knew then the full meaning of our mortal lot, as otherwise he could not have known it, and, knowing that, died in amazement. (*CNT*, 170-71)

Nevertheless, More accepts many of the events of the gospels, together with the whole of their eschatology, only as symbolic expressions of what he considers the facts of the spiritual life.

Judicial appraisal of historical evidence, More claims, shows it to be fact that Jesus lived and taught in Palestine, preached repentance in view of the coming of the kingdom of God, announced himself to be the Messiah, and died on the cross. Much of the rest that we know of Him is conjecture. At the beginning of His life, He most likely had no full consciousness of any divine mission; but as He grew in experience, in knowledge of the expectations of His people, and in consciousness of His own powers, He came to a sense of His mission and announced that the coming of the kingdom was imminent and that He Himself was the Messiah. While there is some doubt about the exact nature of the kingdom He preached, it was at least "the sphere of God's rule" (81); and repentance was the preparation for it. This kingdom did not appear, however, in the form in which it had been depicted in the mythology of the Jews, and the growth of religion since the time of Jesus "has been the slow 'de-eschatologizing' of Christianity" (83), a double process which More finds originating in the writings of St. Paul and St. John.

For St. Paul, More has a strong dislike; he is repelled by the Apostle's egotism, by his doctrine, and by the exaggerated emphasis which history has given him. More was once prompted to comment by the accident of having read St. Paul and Theodore Dreiser on the same day: "The two men are alike in one respect, I don't like either of them; but Dreiser is offensive."[2] More had no doubt of the profundity of St. Paul's religion, but he objected that whereas Jesus had drawn His inspiration from the canonical prophets, St. Paul had been formed on the rabbinical speculations of his age and had misinterpreted his Master. In trying to explain to the satisfaction of reason the process by which man is saved through the death and Resurrection of Christ, St.

Paul arrived at the belief that God voluntarily pardons the sinner of his guilt. Then, aware of the objections to this belief, he further rationalized the mystery into a doctrine of election according to which an omnipotent Deity predetermines men for damnation or salvation, restricting His compassion to a small, chosen band. Such a belief reduces man to the level of a purely passive subject and makes justice a matter of arbitrary whim. While St. Paul is to be credited with having made Christianity a religion of faith, it was in this error of "pure theology" (207), the most deplorable aspect of his speculations, that he had his great influence on the Church; it was he who first brought to Christianity "the old Stoic mischief of determinism and liberty" which has plagued the theology of the West since St. Augustine revived it. In contrast, the great Fathers of the East passed over the question of grace and free will and "concentrated almost exclusively on the dogma of the Incarnation" (210).

If St. Paul continues the eschatological emphasis of the synoptic gospels, enlarging their supernatural aspects and concentrating on the Crucifixion and the Resurrection, St. John has virtually no eschatology and presents Christ not as the Messiah whose return is imminently expected, but "as the Logos, whose life on earth is only one incident in the eternal self-revelation of God." Faith too, which in St. Paul had been Hebraic, takes in St. John "the colour of Greek philosophy and Alexandrian *gnôsis*" (211-12). While maintaining against the Gnostics, probably a powerful heresy by the time the fourth gospel was written, that Christ is both the Son of God and truly human, St. John reveals the influence of the Gnostics in his distinction "between the children of light and the sons of darkness" (218). The influence of Greek philosophy is seen in his emphasis on the Word. In the narrative passages of his gospel he uses miracles to prove the divine authority of Jesus, but he also shows that, when Jesus speaks for Himself, He bases His authority not on the miraculous nature of His acts "but on the saving power of what he says" (217)—on words rather than on works.

This apparent inconsistency More explains by the hypothesis that the author of the fourth gospel has constructed his account out of two traditions of Christ; as a result, he embedded the speeches—the Logia—of one tradition in the narrative of another, although the Logia themselves are somewhat inconsistent in style. Thus, we have in St. John's gospel a narrative element which corresponds to that of the gospel of St. Mark, a body of rambling discourses attributed to Jesus but written in the naive, garrulous style of "the loving and beautiful old age of an untrained intellect" (222)—perhaps the intellect of St. John himself—and coming to the evangelist through some oral or written tradition comparable to the sources of St. Matthew and St. Luke; but scattered through these discourses are passages which "derive from a deeper source and a finer brain" (223)—the "sayings of Jesus himself" (225). Finally, this work of the evangelist has been edited by some third person "who perceived clearly the drift of the Logia, grasped their inmost spirit, and expressed this in language borrowed from the philosophical schools of Alexandria" (233); the Prologue is the work of this editor. It is crucial to More's analysis of St. John's gospel and to his interpretation of the whole Greek tradition that the true drift of the Logia, and especially of the authentic sayings of Jesus, was to emphasize His otherworldliness, His divinity, and His eternality.

Thus, More concludes, the Messianic claims reported in the synoptic gospels are in truth the claims of Jesus, but they have undoubtedly undergone some modification in the recording. Jesus "did veritably acknowledge himself to be the Christ, the Son of the Blessed, whom the men of his own generation should behold sitting on the right hand of power and coming in the clouds of heaven" (247). Yet He did not come. Are we to conclude then that He was deluded? In a sense perhaps He was, but only because, being a man of His times and having been molded by the traditions of His people, He spoke in their language and thought in terms of the Messianic tradition of the prophets. But beyond the Messianic claims we have His other claims to speak with "a spiritual authority of a different order" and beyond this, in the gospel of St. John, the legitimate interpretation of these claims, which were veiled in the speech of the Galilean Jesus. These spiritual claims were not exaggerated but authentic, and they contain something the prophets never said or heard. If Jesus was deluded, the delusion is insignificant.

More's refusal to accept the eschatology of the New Testament except as it symbolizes such general truths as the existence of the otherworld, the constant imminence of death, and the responsibility of every man for his actions (87-88) is consistent with his treatment of miracles. Assuming the position of the skeptic who admits the existence of two realms of being but cannot explain their coalescence, More will not preclude the possibility of miracles. He is personally indifferent to them and would rather say nothing about them, but he concedes that two of them, the Virgin Birth and the Resurrection, are so closely related to the very nature of Jesus as to require some attention. The Virgin Birth he dismisses as an invention of late origin that is unsupported by either scriptural authority or by logical necessity; and he denies the Resurrection insofar as it means literally that Christ's mortal body came back to life. More concedes something to the Resurrection, though precisely what is difficult to say. This event was not a literal rising from the dead, nor did it come about because Jesus had not truly died, nor was it the report of persons suffering hallucination. The meetings of the disciples with the risen Jesus, rather, were "manifestations of spirit to spirit, the warranty of knowledge, based on miraculous intervention, that he whom they mourned as dead was living with God, their Saviour and victorious King, the dispenser of the Holy Ghost" (279)—a confirmation of some sort of the one essential mystery, the Incarnation.

It is worth noting, about such passages, that More does not explain away the miracle as the invention, conscious or unconscious, of those who reported it. Rather, like Hawthorne in his novels and tales, he reports what is said to have happened but neither assents to the literal truth of the account, which stretches the credulity of a rational man, nor denies it, because it contains a truth which is more important than the truth of superficial fact and which imparts to the fact a quality of the sacrosanct. Considering the miracle of the Transfiguration, to take another example, he writes: "It is idle to inquire into the exact nature of what happened, or to apply the prosaic instrument of psychology to its interpretation; still more futile to dimiss it as pure fiction" (157).

The better minds of the Hellenistic age—so runs the argument of *Christ the Word*—were drawn to Christianity because they were dissatisfied with the crudities of Hellenistic superstition and were not quite satisfied with the remote inferences of Plato's religion. When they came upon the gospel of St. John with its message of the Word made flesh, it seemed that all the difficulties of the Platonic ideas—of how they were imminent in the terrestrial world—fell away. The fourth gospel's merging of Platonism and Christianity was equally a benefit to Christianity, for it marks that compromise with the wisdom of the world without which the new religion would have found it difficult to spread itself into the West.

More sees three phases in the development of Christianity from an obscure Oriental religion to a doctrine acceptable to the sophisticated Western mind: repulsion of the attacks of the pagans, victory over Gnosticism, and the elimination of heresy from within. The first achievement was the work of the early apologists, Justin, Clement of Rome, Ignatius, and Athenagoras; the second, of the theosophists, Irenaeus, Clement of Alexandria, and Origen; the third, of Athanasius, Cyril, and the great Cappadocians. Although the conflict with the Gnostics proved, chiefly through the work of Clement, that Christianity was "the legitimate heir of Platonism" (91), More's interest is primarily in the heresies of the third phase, which led to the pronouncements of Nicea and Chalcedon.

Despite the importance which the doctrine of the Trinity would eventually assume, More points out, it was only of secondary importance in the early Church. It entered Christianity, he believes, through the influence of other mythologies in which a triad of deities was a common feature; and although it had become a tenet of orthodoxy by the early years of the third century, the Greek mind assimilated it only a century or more later, after much protest and under the urging of the Western Church. But the entire Church held from the beginning that Christ was a separate person both human and divine. The central problem of theology was therefore not that of the Trinity but that of reconciling the divinity of the Second Person with the monotheism of the Old Testament. In the same way, the heresies of the early Church were Incarnational heresies.

What the Church should have done, in the face of opposition to the conception of the "duality of persons" (131) in the one God, was to affirm the paradox and leave it a mystery. Compromising instead with the language of the schools, she rationalized the definition and thereby invited a proliferation of other definitions by the major heresiarchs of the day who were all intent upon reconciling the doctrine with a monistic theism. The Incarnational heresies—the Sabellian, the Arian, the Nestorian, and the Monophysite heresies—came in two distinct periods corresponding respectively to two phases in the development of the dogma. Sabellianism and Arianism were opposing attempts to reconcile belief in one God with belief in Jesus Christ as both fully divine and separate from the Father: the Sabellians accepted the divinity of the Logos but not its separate personality; the Arians, the personality of the Logos but not the full divinity. Against these the Council of Nicea in 325 affirmed both the true divinity and the separate personality of the Logos. Nestorianism and Monophysitism were attempts to reconcile the true humanity with the true divinity of Christ: the Nestorians explained that Christ was two persons, one human, one divine; and the Monophysites denied the humanity of Christ. Against these the Church declared at Chalcedon in 451 that Christ was one person possessing two natures.

One of the arguments More uses to support his view that the doctrine of the Incarnation is the one essential doctrine of Christianity is taken from the declaration of faith issued at Nicea in 325. The Council at one point in its deliberations agreed on a creed put forth by Eusebius of Caesarea; but for some reason now lost to history, it adopted one which differed substantially from the creed of Eusebius, chiefly in omitting a clause which affirmed a distinctly Trinitarian doctrine. There is no doubt in More's mind that those attending the Council believed in the Trinity; he supposes that the modification of the creed of Eusebius came about simply because the question of the divinity of Christ overshadowed all others. But whatever the motive of the Fathers at the Council of Nicea, the effect was that "from that day to this . . . Christianity is coterminus with a full and unequivocal acceptance of the Incarnation, with its single antecedent, belief in God the Father and Creator, and its essential corollary, belief in the resurrection and in the communion of God through the spirit" (158-59).

Furthermore, despite the rather abstract quality of the term *homoousios*,[3] the definition of Nicea was not intended to enforce a mere metaphysical subtlety; it was, on the contrary, a safeguard against the encroachment of metaphysical reason on the simplicity of religion. Of all the definitions put forth at the time, only the anti-metaphysical definition which the Council adopted could have preserved Christianity from sinking into unimportance. Hence, it was no mere question of terminology that the Council decided but the very fate of Christianity. "It is inconceivable that a humanitarian religion should have conquered the world" (173).

Like the debates of Nicea, the debates of Chalcedon have the appearance of being a quarrel over terms, but their purpose and their effect were simply to restate the *homoousios* of the Nicene definition and to make explicit the inevitable corollary of that definition, that the incarnate Christ remains one person but has assumed a second nature. What is most important is that the Council of Chalcedon did not go beyond the mere affirmation of the dogma into an explanation of it or of its terms. It is thus "a singular event in the annals of theology" (193). Before Chalcedon the heretics in one way or another sought to impose their metaphysical speculations on the divine mystery. After Chalcedon, particularly with the advent of scholasticism, the general councils themselves fell into error by committing the Church "to a theological method implicitly heretical" (195-96). For this reason, the Council of Chalcedon is the end of the Greek tradition. Plato prepared for a religion "based on the Word made flesh" (267), and "the Greek Fathers at Chalcedon may be said to have set their seal on the long tradition which took its rise in Athens exactly to the year eight centuries and a half before they met" (267).

IV *The Middle Way*

Unlike its predecessors in *The Greek Tradition*, *The Catholic Faith* is not the analysis of a philosophical system or of a continuous historical development. It is a volume of relatively independent essays on Buddhism, the Apostles' Creed, the Church, the Eucharist, and Christian mysticism—or, to stress the unity of the book, on some of the doctrinal implications of the Incarnation and some forms of the religious life which More regards as rivals to the Catholic faith.

While he believes that it is possible to consider most non-Christian religions as primitive gropings toward the reality best revealed in Christianity, he finds it somewhat more difficult thus to account for Buddhism. Like Christianity, Buddhism claims to be the perfect way, stresses otherworldliness and moral responsibility, and originates in the teachings of a noble, gracious, and imperious figure. Its most fundamental difference from Christianity is that it denies the existence of God and of the human soul. In discussing the strength and the weakness of Buddhism, both of which spring from the dualism of the system, More distinguishes two types of dualism. Absolute dualism postulates a radical distinction between spirit and matter, good and evil. Though rationally incomprehensible—the argument will by now be familiar—this distinction is known to our consciousness, and its serves as the basis of reasonable inference; without it, neither religion nor morality corresponds to any objective reality. An "absolved dualism" (*CF*, 66) holds to the same distinction of spirit and matter, but with the difference that spirit can attain to a condition of complete unity and changelessness in which it is absolutely free of involvement in materiality or the flux. Such a condition is the goal of all mysticism, and Buddhism affirms it with particular logic and force. It is, however, simply another metaphysical illusion which corresponds to nothing within the range of certain knowledge. The end of Buddhism, the Parinirvâna, is not an end of the moral life in the sense of a consummation; it is simply a total negation into which the soul passes, carrying with it nothing of either earthly or heavenly experience. It renders meaningless the entire moral life. Buddhism is therefore best seen, like other religions, as "a preface to the Gospel, . . . the most convincing argument withal that truth to be clearly known waits upon revelation" (75). As for Christian mysticism, which would also fall under the objections More makes to Neoplatonic mysticism in *Hellenistic Philosophies,* it is a fanatic withdrawal from a full —and thus a true—human life.

In contrast both to Buddhism and to Christian mysticism, the doctrine of Christ, properly understood and followed, satisfies all the demands of the soul; since it therefore speaks with the authority of conscience, we may take it as "the distinctive authority of revelation" (173). Yet, while we are certain of the principles of true religion as they are enunciated by Christ, we are frequently uncertain of how they apply in specific situations. This insufficiency precludes our accepting the gospels as an absolute revelation and leads to the necessity of regarding religion as a matter of both individual understanding and tradition. Recognizing the limitations of our own intelligence and being at the same time impressed with the weight of historical tradition, we hesitate to reject the formulations of an institutional religion in favor of private authority alone—especially since we know that religion can be kept alive only within some corporate worship. But knowing also that we must satisfy the demands of our own consciences and willy nilly judge for ourselves, we are justified in maintaining our own interpretation of the doctrines of any religious body in whose worship we participate. It is in such a spirit that More himself accepts the Incarnation and the other doctrines of the creeds—not in the sense the words held for their formulators or successive generations of Christians, but in a sense compatible with the knowledge of his own age and with his own understanding of things. While such reservations resemble hypocrisy, he thinks that he is sufficiently preserved from hypocrisy if he can give "whole-hearted assent" to a truth behind the "metaphorical language" of a creed (111).

The ideal of religion, therefore, is "a kind of revelation which neither in book nor in Church is absolute, but in both book and Church possesses a sufficient authority" (183). An absolute Church argues *a priori* from theoretical pretensions; an authoritative one is pragmatic, instilling religion into the world but avoiding both the chaos of Protestant individualism and the absolutism of Rome. There are no essays in *The Catholic Faith* which directly discuss Protestant individualism, but "The Church" aims explicitly at undermining "the Roman stronghold" (181) by showing how the doctrine of papal infallibility "must cause a complete rupture between a religion so committed and any reasonable philosophy of life" (188). Anglicanism, More believes, avoids "the excesses of Romanist and Radical Protestant," preserving "the just balance between fundamentals and accessories which was threatened by an authority vested in the infallibility whether of Tradition or of Scripture."[4] For this reason, and perhaps influenced also by his conviction that the English Church since the Renaissance had been turning from the great medieval and Reformation theologians to the Greek Fathers of the early Church (*RP*, ix), More considered himself an Anglican, although his individualism was strong enough to keep him from being confirmed in the Anglican or Episcopalian communion.[5]

How far More had come from the religious convictions of the *Shelburne Essays* can be seen from his essay on Newman (*SE*, VIII, 39-79). It was Newman's misfortune, he wrote, to have been born in an age when belief in religious authority could be maintained only at the cost of violence to the mind of the believer. Newman "might have accepted manfully the sceptical demolition of the Christian mythology and the whole fabric of external religion, and on the ruins of such creeds he might have risen to that supreme insight which demands no revelation and is dependent on no authority, but is content within itself"; or, adhering "to the national worship as a symbol of the religious experience of the people," he might, by infusing into that worship the vitality of true religion, have helped prepare his people to accept a religion divested of external forms. Strong enough for neither course, Newman distorted the facts of his religious experience "to make them agree with a physical revelation," thereby rejecting the mission of faith (74-75).

At the time of this essay, in 1913, More had himself made the first of the two choices he holds out to Newman: he had accepted the "demolition of the Christian mythology" and come to rest on his own insight. He would never go so far as Newman in his acceptance of external authority; he continued to believe that Newman had been "frightened . . . into the prison-house of absolutism."[6] Yet More would come to admit that Newman meant more to him than any other writer of the nineteenth century[7] and that he had originally condemned Newman because Newman had become a Roman Catholic rather than a Brahmin ("Marginalia," 27). By 1936, the date of this admission, More regarded his whole quest for a "pure religion," which had engaged him all through the *Shelburne Essays,* as "a harmless concession to the truth of some spiritual abstractions which supposedly can elevate and pacify the soul without intruding any claims on our intellect or any authority over our personal liberty" ("Marginalia," 7). The philosophy he had derived from the Upanishads led to "an impossible transcendental monism, and *The Catholic Faith* is my public retractation of what can be read in some of my earlier books."[8]

One of the most widely read of all More's works is *The Sceptical Approach to Religion,* whose purpose is to show that a consistent and honest use of reason should lead the skeptic to a receptive attitude toward religious doctrine. Far more compact than the six-volume *Greek Tradition,* it is perhaps the most convenient introduction to the religious and philosophical aspect of Paul Elmer More—both the writings and the man. It is a capsule presentation of his Platonism, of his biblical criticism, of his views on the Incarnation; it also reveals the author as a man at once learned, confident, reverent, and humble.

Admitting the charge of the agnostic that faith is a kind of wish-belief, More insists in *The Sceptical Approach* that it is also a way of life fashioned on belief and, further, that the agnostic cannot merely suspend his belief but must either accept the inference of faith with its practical consequences or, denying the inference of faith, accept the practical consequences of his denial. But the universal experience of man is that the conception of a godless or purposeless universe is fraught with despair and resentment. All things considered, "the so-called disbelief of the infidel is an inference which, if honestly examined, demands an act of almost impossible credulity" (25). Then, arguing more positively from both the philosophy of Plato and the findings of modern biblical criticism, More comes to the same conclusion about the meaning of the Incarnation that he reaches in *The Greek Tradition*. When we outgrow our fascination with the higher criticism's discovery of the common elements in the world's religions, a more disinterested criticism will see that the monotheistic current which runs through the great religions has worked itself out only in the Judaeo-Christian tradition. So impressive a fact must be explained by a commensurate cause. In addition, the event of the Incarnation is merely a confirmation in history of the psychological experience of the individual. It has, therefore, the appearance of being a divine confirmation of a fact impressed upon men by a number of experiences, both personal and historical. None of this argument coercively demonstrates the uniqueness and the truth of Christianity, but it is a stronger body of evidence, as "the honest sceptic will admit" (158), than the conviction of the individual believer. It is as if God had burst into the world in answer to man's groping aspirations. "Considering the objective means whereby God makes known His nature and will, I for one simply cannot conceive a further step in the scale of revelation beyond the historic event of the Word made flesh" (167).

V *Critique of* The Greek Tradition

While the author of such a work as *The Greek Tradition* can hardly disclaim the intention of writing history, the primary intention which More describes in *Platonism* and to which he adheres through the five succeeding volumes is to write not a history, but what might better be called a protrepticus, an invitation to the practice of philosophy. Further, he hopes that those searching for an intellectual center in the meaningless gropings of modern thought will find some appeal in his work. *The Greek Tradition* is thus philosophy and polemics as well as history. As philosophy, it continues the search for personal satisfaction which we have seen in his other writings; as polemics, it is part of his fight against that inclusive enemy, naturalism. Those who would oppose "the threatening tide of dissolution and materialism," he writes in *Christ the Word,* must recover the religious tradition that runs from Socrates to the Council of Chalcedon, clean it of superstition, and make it "a rallying point for the best thought of our time as it was for the best thought of the past" (7).

We have seen how More in *Aristocracy and Justice* identifies the problem of twentieth-century democracy with the problem that Plato faced in the democracy of fourth-century Athens, and how his criticisms of progressive politics, university education, demagoguery, humanitarianism, pragmatism, the compromising of the Churches, the betrayal of leadership by the upper classes, and all the other evils he found in his society rest on what he finds in Plato. Conversely, modern naturalism in its various forms is in his mind all through *The Greek Tradition* and *The Sceptical Approach to Religion.* "The condemnation of the sophists," he writes in *Platonism,* is "that they were themselves so deeply immersed in the popular tide, and lent their weight to its onward sweep" (25)—precisely the charge he levels at Theodore Roosevelt and the intellectual and moral leaders of his own day. In Plato he finds direct refutations of "the scientific conception of a 'block universe,'" of Spencer, and of "the various forms of Pragmatism, . . . including the much bruited metaphysic of M. Bergson" (*P,* 263). The opinion of Thrasymachus in *The Republic* and of Callicles in the *Gorgias* to the effect "that justice is the interest of the stronger, and nothing more," men "now in this latter age are hearing proclaimed as a novel doctrine by teachers of the Nietzschean type" (*P,* 57-58). In *Hellenistic Philosophies* More draws an analogy between the materialism of Zeno and the Stoics and that of Wordsworth and Thomas Huxley (80-82). In *The Sceptical Approach to Religion* he describes Socrates of the *Phaedo* as expressing "a dissatisfaction with the theories of deterministic evolution derived by his forerunners from the observation of nature" (95). Finally, there are several digressions in the later volumes of *The Greek Tradition* (e.g., *CNT*, 135-38) into the humanitarian religion of the twentieth century.

Undoubtedly Plato anticipates many of the errors of later times; at least one reviewer of *Platonism* has found More's comparisons of Plato and Descartes, Locke, and Edwards worthwhile.[9] Knowing More's obsession with Darwinism, its offspring, and its congeners, we nevertheless see an occasional sophistry in such phrases as "deterministic evolution."

The Greek Tradition was naturally widely reviewed, and by competent Platonists. While these reviewers found much to admire in it and particularly praised its intention of reviving Platonism for the modern world, they also agreed on a number of strictures. They found many errors of historical fact, misinterpretation amounting at times to willful mistranslation of philosophical texts, an exaggeration of minor aspects of Plato's thought, a too exclusively ethical concern and consequent distortion of Plato's ideas on mathematical and scientific matters, an uncritical dualism, an un-Platonic suspicion of logic and "metaphysics," a too-frequent habit of deciding crucial questions by mere pronouncement rather than by the presentation of evidence, and a general tendency to warp Plato to the idiosyncracies of Paul Elmer More.

"On points of scholarship," wrote A. E. Taylor in a review of *Platonism*, "though he is apt to be very magisterial in his deliveries, he usually gives no reasons to speak of for his decisions, and they are not always such as a sound scholar would be likely to accept without misgiving." While "he is always suggestive and often convincing" in his treatment of Plato's ethics, More seriously distorts Plato in minimizing the importance of the philosopher's scientific and mathematical interests, which in fact he may not fully understand.[10] In *The Religion of Plato*, Taylor thought, More's most serious errors are his dualistic reading of Plato's philosophy and religion and his reasoning from psychological to cosmic dualism. Furthermore, "the dogmatic definition of the *persona* Christi [*sic*] has nothing to do with the dualism of the human soul."[11]

Virtually repeating the criticisms of Taylor, John Burnet attacks *Platonism* for its ignorance of historical fact and its exaggeration or misinterpretation of minor elements in Plato. More "is too apt to dispose of difficulties by a mere *ipse dixit,* and he has not a very firm grasp of the history of Greek thought." One of the numerous matters on which he is in error is his interpretation of Socrates' *daimon* to be an ethical voice when it is merely a premonition of undesirable consequences.[12] Describing *Platonism* as belonging to "the old type of Platonic philology which substitutes the combination of keynote sentences for a flexible literary and philosophical analysis of the entire course of the thought," Paul Shorey accuses More of imposing on the clear language of Plato a "vocabulary of mysticism and irrationality." Plato makes no use of the idea of intuition, nor does anything in him correspond to More's distinction between "the lower and the higher reason."[13]

In a more general study of More's Platonism than any of these reviewers attempts, William D. Geoghegan[14] describes *The Greek Tradition* as an oversimplified, arbitrary presentation of Plato that is "thoroughly unreliable" and distorted by "a moralistic and obscurantist dualism" (45). By seeing the culmination of Platonism in the Council of Chalcedon, More creates a gap of fifteen hundred years in the history of that philosophy and implies that it lay obscured and corrupted until he revived it. His derivation of Plato's ontological and epistemological dualism from "a subjective moral dualism" (42-43), his notion that the Platonic ideas are imaginative projections of moral data, his contention that Plato resorted to myth and theology because he despaired of finding answers to religious questions in philosophy, and his description of Plato's God are unwarranted by anything in Plato.

If these criticisms of More's Platonism by scholars like Taylor, Burnet, and Shorey seem to discredit *The Greek Tradition*, that impression must not be left to stand. A scholar trained in the historical, textual, philosophical, and other technical aspects of his study is perhaps justified in treating the non-professional's inaccuracies in specific detail while expressing respect for the non-professional's accomplishment in more general terms; the accomplishment is there nonetheless. In thus referring to More as a non-professional, I do not mean to imply that his work does not merit the attention of the professional; More would certainly have disclaimed such immunity. I mean that, in spite of his enormous erudition and the scrupulousness of his scholarship, he did not have the full technical competence or the interest in minutiae of the specialist. When, while teaching at Princeton

University in the 1920's, he transferred from philosophy to the classics, he did so, according to A. H. Dakin, "chiefly because . . . he was not a 'professional' philosopher—not a Doctor of Philosophy of the then Teutonic type."[15]

A distinction Thoreau makes toward the beginning of *Walden* is also relevant: "There are nowadays professors of philosophy, but not philosophers." More is not the professor, but the philosopher; not simply the student of Plato, but the disciple. Though he was undoubtedly swayed by personal bias on this point or that, his purpose was to demonstrate the central moral and religious significance of Plato's thought. That significance is not to be discovered by ignoring the text; to the extent that More is careless or inaccurate or that he distorts the text, he merits censure. But in the words of Whitney J. Oates, classical scholar and student of philosophy, "Whatever criticisms may be levelled in one way or another against More's analysis of Plato's basic thought, . . . it cannot be denied that it expresses in bold outline the position which is given in the text of the dialogues."[16]

More's interpretation of Christianity received much the same reception as his interpretation of Platonism; in general, reviewers admired its intent and its spirit but questioned its doctrinal and historical accuracy. Austin Warren, though he finds fault with *Christ the Word* because of its treatment of the Holy Ghost in the early church, welcomes the book as the record of More's discovery of Christianity. But while More leans toward Catholicism rather than toward Protestantism, Warren points out, he professes no allegiances; and after distinguishing between the Roman and the Anglican Churches, More speaks of the Catholic Church without defining quite what he means. "One of the most valuable, as it is surely one of the most authoritative, parts of *Christ the Word*" is the attempt to show that the doctrine of the Logos is a fulfillment of Plato.[17] Geoghegan, on the other hand, describing the similarities More finds between Platonism and Christianity as "superficial and obvious," sees More's belief that Chalcedon confirmed Platonism as "simply a notion" unsupported by either historical or rational evidence; More's "Binitarianism," like his idea that matter is the evil necessity resisting divine purposes, is also a "quasi-Manichean notion" (50-51). Fr. Martin D'Arcy, S.J., finds *The Catholic Faith* "harsh," "dogmatic," a book not "about the Catholic faith" but "an expression of what Mr.

More would like that faith to be"—though the critic does not feel the need for detailed refutation.[18]

Against the Roman Catholic Church More uses a tactic he has previously used against the social reformers of the twentieth century; he presents its case in the worst light and imputes to it positions which it does not in fact hold. He charges in *The Catholic Faith* that the doctrine of papal infallibility has committed Rome to a method of biblical interpretation substantially the same as that of the fundamentalist Protestant sects; has "narrowed down the instrument of inspiration . . . to the *ex cathedra* utterance of the one bishop who occupies the throne of St. Peter"—a phrase which soon becomes "to the judgement of one old man after another"—and has thus "set up for our credence the sharpest and most brittle Absolute the world has ever known"; has imposed upon all men of whatever age the obligation of subscribing to dogmas "for which not an iota of authority can be drawn from the original *depositum fidei*; and "has committed herself, again irrevocably, to a medieval outgrowth of superstition which goes far in the direction of converting the sacraments into feats of magic" (191-93).

These strictures are made in the essay "The Church," in which More argues that modern man can retain both "his faith as a Christian and his integrity of mind" only if he conceives of revelation as "authoritative without being absolute, and reasonable without being rationalistic" (171). The twin enemies of this same middle way are the fundamentalist Protestant's faith in an infallible Bible and the Roman Catholic's faith in an infallible Church. Because More believes that biblical fundamentalists "have lost their cause so utterly and finally that nothing can add to their discomfiture" (180), "The Church" discusses only Rome.

By confining its claims of infallibility to the spheres of faith and morals, More writes, by conceding its fallibility in all but *ex cathedra* pronouncements, and by being vague about which of its pronouncements are *ex cathedra* and which are not, Rome has made her position difficult to attack. But if we forgo theoretical objections to her claims and look instead at her history, we find the practical weakness of her position. Her doctrines are based on the most ambiguous passages of Scripture; institutions, like the episcopacy, which she traces back to Christ and the Apostles actually developed later, almost "from the accidental needs of the clerical organization" (185); not only have the papacy and the clergy fallen at times into corruption, but the Popes have on occasion preached doctrines so close to heresy, even from the Roman point of view, as to be distinguished from it only by a quibble.

In spite of these criticisms, More concedes "the great merit and the magnificent achievement of the Roman Church" (197). She was unwaveringly defended the doctrine of the Incarnation "as the supreme fact of history" and the central tenet of theology. Through the continuity and the universal appeal of her liturgy, at the center of which stands the Eucharistic sacrifice of the Mass, a manifestation of the Incarnation, she justifies her claim to catholicity.

Some of the strongest objections More makes to the authoritarianism of Rome rest on what he takes to be the logical implications of Roman Catholic dogmas. For a man who praised the Fathers of Nicea and Chalcedon because they simply pronounced their dogmas and avoided both the definition of dogmatic terms and the drawing out of logical implications, such objections are somewhat inconsistent. While there are unavoidable implications of some sort in every dogma, dogma, as More knew, is essentially the defining of a belief for the sole purpose of preserving it from corruption, not for that of implying some other belief. The dogmatist says, in effect, "That is what I believe, and I will not speculate upon it further"; there is nothing to the dogmatic intent but what is explicit. More's rejoinder might be that the dogmas defined at Nicea and Chalcedon are formulations of the one essential truth of Christianity, that they are rooted firmly in the Scriptures, and that later dogmas of Rome are not. Still, when he objects to a dogma on grounds of its alleged logical implications, he is making an irrelevant objection.

The significant implications of dogma are not those merely potential ones which can be detected by logic, but those which as a matter of fact develop in the course of time. Of all the possible implications in a given dogma, some may become historically significant, others will not. Those which do may become themselves the occasions of other definitions. More understood this process well enough, since he traces, in *Christ the Word,* the course whereby certain implications of the dogma defined at Nicea in 325 led to the definition of Chalcedon in 451. Something of the dangers of seeing logical implications where none in fact exist can be illustrated by what is probably the most naive piece of reasoning that ever took place in the mind of Paul Elmer More. The doctrine of the Immaculate Conception, he says in *The Catholic Faith,* "implies that, if the Mother of Christ is to be held without sin, then her parents must have been exempt from the curse of transmitting the taint of original sin in the act of conceiving her; and this in good logic would require that the parents of her parents enjoyed the same exception, and so on backwards *ad Adamum*" (193). In other words, original sin is transmitted through the genes.

It is not difficult to discover why More is so scrupulous in avoiding the logical implications of the Incarnation and so free in ascribing implications elsewhere. His argument in *Christ the Word* against the Holy Ghost's equality with the Father and the Son is based on syntactical analysis of biblical passages from which the doctrine is derived and upon the alleged unauthenticity of those passages; but his chief objection, when all is said, is the obverse of his reason for accepting the Incarnation. The equality of the Father and the Son symbolizes and confirms the dualism of his own consciousness, and the Holy Ghost does not fit in. The doctrine of the Trinity "tends to conceal the true nature and function of the spirit as the power of God manifesting Himself in the world" (130); it "deprives the New Testament of its most exquisite and beautiful symbol of the intercommunion of the spirit of God and the spirit of man, for 'know ye not that ye are the temple of God, and that the Spirit of God dwelleth in you?'" (338).

VI *"the quest of God"*

According to T. S. Eliot, "More's works are, in the deepest sense, his autobiography."[19] It has been my contention all along that the underlying unity of More's work was his own search for truth and that his writings, whatever other purposes they have, are the expression of what he found. If we are mindful of the objections to *The Greek Tradition* which I have summarized above, we may perhaps see an irony in Eliot's statement; it is an irony, I think, which More himself would have acknowledged. "I cannot escape an uneasy doubt," he wrote in regard to the argument of *Platonism,* "that it is a waste of energy to attempt to express in the logical terms of reason what ought really to be left in the vague penumbra of the feelings—that, perhaps, the sort of truth I have been endeavoring to define ceases to be truth as soon as it is defined."[20] But no irony can be found in what Eliot says immediately after the remark I have just quoted from him: "One is always aware of the sincerity, and in the later works the Christian humility (a very rare virtue too) of the concentrated mind seeking God."

The most directly personal account of More's search for God is contained in *Pages from an Oxford Diary,* a small volume purporting to be the diary of an Oxford don but actually, as More's preface assures us, "the transcription of a very real experience of my own." Written at Oxford during his European journey of 1924-1925, the manuscript of the volume was discovered by his daughter Darrah about a month before his death in 1937. Urged by his friend Whitney J. Oates to publish it, More made some changes and additions, dictated a preface, and sent it to the press.[21] It appeared shortly after his death.

Pages from an Oxford Diary surveys the intellectual development we have already reviewed—More's early romanticism, his first serious interest in literature, his materialism, the smoldering under all this of "the hidden fire which was kindled in my soul at birth" (sec. VI), his Hinduism, and finally his conviction "that I shall end my days a conscious, as I was born, an unconscious, Platonist" (sec. VI). There are brief discussions of Newman, St. Augustine, and other religious figures of greater or lesser importance to him and passing comments on Darwinism and other metaphysical errors. But the volume is chiefly concerned with the mixed certainties and uncertainties of its author's present hard-won beliefs—with the perplexities, more specifically, of a faith unsupported, even opposed, by reason. "The question of a God must be answered by direct experience, or by the sort of inference which is rightly called faith. The office of reason resembles that of the *advocatus diaboli* in the creation of saints: is that direct experience or that inference so strong that it persists against and through all endeavours of reason to prove it illusory?" (sec. IX). More's later faith was born one day when, viewing the valley of the Severn, he concluded that such beauty could exist only as the work of a designing intellect. The conclusion, he admits, was neither striking nor original, but it came to him almost with the force of conversion. He still supposes that the argument from design, although no proof, is probably the strongest argument for the existence of God.

In matters of doctrine, he is an individualist. The doctrine of "a static and eternal heaven and hell" outrages his sense of justice, although he knows of no "new symbolism" to "fill the void" (sec. XIII). "Timeless eternity is a bubble of language" (sec. XVI). He does believe that "any true philosophy of God demands the Incarnation" (sec. XXI), but his interpretation of that doctrine and the corollaries he sees in it are not always orthodox. One of these corollaries is that the Incarnation is "no accident in the divine economy, but . . . a deliberately accepted condition of imposing order upon chaos" (sec. XXII)—which is to say that God is a finite being whose purposes are obstructed by some dark necessity and whose descent into human nature is in some mysterious way the price He must pay for the working out of those purposes. Another is that the Father, together with the Son, "suffered in the act of the world's salvation" (sec. XXIII). More was long kept from accepting the truth of Christianity, he admits, by his distaste for the doctrine of the Redemption, which offended either his philosophy or his pride. But age and experience, impressing him with the weakness of all mankind, have brought him to his present state. "The whole current of my thoughts has set in one direction; all my being has become absorbed in the quest of God, and a realization of that spirit world of which He is the Lord and Master" (sec. V):

> And so I sit and wait, in patience and serenity—for the end which is no end. I turn over in my mind the various possibilities of the long journey, amusing myself with fancies that I trust are not purely fanciful. Only of this I am assured, that some time and in some way, spirit to spirit, face to face, I shall meet the great Lord of life, and, falling before Him, tell my gratitude for all He has done, and implore pardon for all I have left undone.

> > For thou wilt not abandon my soul to the grave;
> > In thy presence is fulness of joy,
> > At thy right hand are pleasures for evermore.
> >   (Sec. XXXIII)

CHAPTER 5

Humanism and Naturalism

THE LITERARY CRITICISM of the *New Shelburne Essays*, a series More began in 1928 after having published no collected criticism for over seven years, sweepingly condemns the literature of the twentieth century. In the *Shelburne Essays* and in the other uncollected criticism which he was writing at the same time, his attitude toward contemporary literature was ironic, condescending, and disgusted, perhaps even arrogant; in the *New Shelburne Essays* it is all of these, but impatient and petulant as well. It is as if More had passed from one phase of his criticism to another, had ended his "history of human thought and ideals" in order to begin an attack on modern literature. It was his own recognition of the change that prompted him, as he was preparing his twelfth volume of collected essays, to begin a new series rather than to continue the old. The title *New Shelburne Essays* is a compromise maintaining continuity with the former series but at the same time acknowledging the "somewhat new character" of the new one.[1]

I The Demon of the Absolute

The title of the first volume, *The Demon of the Absolute*, also reflects this continuity, since absolutism was the demon of the *Shelburne Essays* too, even if no title called attention to it, and the title essay of that first volume traces the aberrations of modern literature, philosophy, and natural science to a common root in rationalistic monism. The "somewhat new character" is determined by the moral and philosophical assumptions More finds in the literature of the twentieth century. That literature, like much of the literature he had criticized in the *Shelburne Essays,* is naturalistic; but its sentimental or romantic aspects have been replaced by a harsh brutality.

The distractions of modern life, More writes in the Preface to *The Demon of the Absolute*—and this notion is hardly peculiar to the new series—are traceable to the immersion of man in the stream of nature which originated with Bacon. In the Aristotelian scheme, man was both in nature and above it; with Bacon, there arose a tendency to see man only as a natural creature governed by the forces which govern all natural things and to ignore the self-determining supernaturalism of his humanity. Two principal errors have resulted. One is the extension of scientific thought which reached its climax in the nineteenth century and which teaches that the universe runs forever under the governance of mechanical laws. The other is our fear that this same universe, far from being the tight machine Newtonian physics has taken it to be, is an infinite and impermanent flux without purpose or meaning. Both errors deny the reality of anything outside the stream of nature, and both deprive life of any serious interest.

More had rather thoroughly examined the first of these errors in the *Shelburne Essays*, and there are references to it in the *New Shelburne Essays*. But in the new series he is more concerned with the literature of the second—a literature which represents man "as the merely passive channel for an ever-flowing stream of sensations" (*NSE*, I, xi). As in the *Shelburne Essays* he had traced the characteristics of Victorian literature to the scientific conception which then prevailed, so he now traces the "ever-flowing stream" of twentieth-century literature to twentieth-century science. Though none of the *New Shelburne Essays* deals exclusively with science, in a section of "The Demon of the Absolute" entitled "The Phantom of Pure Science" (*NSE*, I, 42-51) More describes how the objective world of material objects, which seems to our common sense so solid and permanent, has now been reduced to a nebulous composite of time, space, value, and relationships—to a state of being no more permanent and solid than psychical events, of which transitoriness is the peculiar quality. In the newest science "the organic and the inorganic worlds flow together in an indistinguishable flux, wherein the soul also, dissolved by association into a complex of relationships, loses that central permanence of entity which used to be held to mark the dignity of man" (49). Such a theory, More believes, is the intellectual stimulus of the new literature of symbolism and its related schools.

II *Twentieth Century Literature*

Two of the most instructive examples of such literature he finds in the works of Proust and Joyce, to each of whom he devotes an essay: "Proust: The Two Ways" (*NSE*, III, 43-68) and "James Joyce" (*NSE*, III, 69-96). Beginning the essay on Proust in a slightly ironical tone, More describes *Remembrance of Things Past* as "portentous" in both its length and its combination of "unity of purpose with dispersion of method" (43); the opening section—by which More means the sections "Overture" and "Combray" of *Swann's Way*—is "the subtlest and truest and most interesting portion," "highly original, often quaint and exquisite," and, best of all, short (45). But since the work is constructed as an uncontrolled association of ideas, More is inclined to judge it largely on the soundness of its psychology, which he finds "in part surprisingly fine and fresh, in part tediously commonplace, in part vitiated by a fundamentally inadequate conception of human nature, in part sheer nonsense" (46). A more penetrating and intelligent exploitation of psychological association is Joyce's *Ulysses*, but More prefers the *Portrait* and *Dubliners* to either *Ulysses* or *Finnegans Wake*. Indeed, the paradox of James Joyce is how the author of these works, notable for their sense of religious values and their subtleties of style, could have descended to "the moral slough" of *Ulysses* and "the linguistic impertinences" of *Finnegans Wake*, which More refers to under the title of *Work in Progress* (70). Joyce is "a great genius expending itself on the propagation of irresponsibility, while the fabric of society is shaken to its foundation" (93). The failure of both Joyce and Proust is that, despite their great skill, their works lead to nothing worthwhile; on the contrary, they illustrate the futility of an art divorced from moral values.

More remarks in the essay on Joyce that the acknowledged forerunners of the literary movement which includes Joyce, Proust, and the modern symbolist poets are three Americans—Poe, Whitman, and Henry James (79). The point is developed in "The Modernism of French Poetry" (*NSE*, III, 97-116), an essay concerned with the moral significance of symbolism and surrealism and with the origins of those movements in Baudelaire, and in *The Study of English Literature*. In symbolism and the more extreme surrealism, thought is a dream state in which the poet records whatever impressions chance to flow through his mind. Whitman's influence on such poetry can be seen in "Song of Myself," where, by depriving the objective world of all intrinsic value and making it only a flowing stream of sensations confronted by the absolute ego of the poet, he first presented that combination of egoism and naturalism out of which Valéry has formulated the rationale of symbolism. Its sources in Poe are equally demonstrable, for in his work too there is something of the same dissolution of the solid world into images of the soul's fluctuations, and his critical writings uphold the ideal of pure beauty toward which the symbolists work. The influence of James is somewhat less direct, but it is important nevertheless.

In the late novels of Henry James the desires and needs of the human soul are presented virtually as conflicting agents within that soul, as independent entities functioning as symbols of the drama in which the character is engaged. James does not dissolve the character into constituent elements, but leaves it as an inclusive entity. Yet if one takes the New England conscience from James's achievement and gives each of the psychological combatants equal freedom and validity, the inner drama of moral issues becomes something else again. The thoughts and fancies flow not from a mind but through it "by a kind of hypnotic suggestion" or free association; then one has "not the dramatized novel but a dissolution of drama in the stream of consciousness." James's own writing may bear more on the method than on the spirit of that device, but it is in the very nature of modern fiction that method and spirit are inseparable, and both Joyce and Gertrude Stein acknowledge James as the founder of modern fiction.[2]

James's method, More believes, is finally self-defeating because it imitates the method of drama but has no dramatic vividness;[3] More questions the intellectual seriousness of those who enjoy it: "A man may have an inordinate subtlety of intellect without ever coming in sight of an idea" (*NSE,* I, 112). More himself never came to terms with James. In 1920 James still lay "in a dim and nebulous mist beyond my astronomy";[4] the following year More declared himself "incompetent" to write an obituary of him.[5] "James seems to me a peculiarly difficult subject. Frankly his novels have never appealed to me. But I recognize that my distaste for him—disgust, in the old sense of the word—is partly due to a trait of indolence in my make-up. It has always been irksome to me to respond to the requirements of acrobatic ingenuity he demands. I have consoled myself with saying *Le jeu ne vaut pas les chandelles.* The same amount of labour would furnish the key to Aristotle—and what after all does James really give one for all one's intellectual toil? Yet I may be wrong, or I may be dull."[6] He held much the same opinion of Proust and Joyce, believing that the enthusiasm of their followers was owing in great measure to a love of the bizarre and the difficult (*NSE*, III, 46-47, 84).

Perhaps the most telling example of More's estrangement from contemporary literature is the difficulty he had with T. S. Eliot. Although he enjoyed "rather an intimate acquaintance" with Eliot,[7] generally shared the poet's views on politics and religion, and had the benefit of long conversations with him on his work,[8] More was never at ease with Eliot's poetry. Eliot once told him that "Ash Wednesday" expressed the purgation of the passions, but More found the information of little help. The poem read well aloud; why couldn't it also be intelligible?[9] More's trouble seems to have been about the same that he had with James—an unwillingness, if not an inability, to meet the formal demands of contemporary literature. Although Eliot had withdrawn from the school of art for art's sake, in which he had written his "criticisms of Shakespeare and Dante preposterously absurd,"[10] "the wild mystifications"[11] of his later poetry showed his continued adherence to its methods. While the effects of his conversion were apparent in his subsequent essays, the techniques of "Ash Wednesday" and the other later poetry better suited the lyricist of chaos than the religious and political conservative.[12] Meeting with objections to this opinion, More tried to clarify it; but in doing so he skirted the question of the intrinsic value of Eliot's poetry. Since Eliot's personal values and his poetic themes were now traditional and orthodox, so should be the form of his poetry; in continuing in his former vein, he is giving comfort to the enemy. A poet must be granted freedom in his choice of form, More admits, but a wrong form can negate what he means to convey: "Eliot has never as an artist come into the open. He still is a leader for radical young men who loathe and detest what he now stands for."[13]

When More was asked in 1926 to contribute an article on modern American literature to *La Revue de Paris,* he once again declared himself incompetent. Dreiser, Cabell, Dos Passos, Lewis, "*et id genus omne*" were undoubtedly one of the chief schools of modern American fiction, but they struck him as "an ungodly sort."[14] It would be easy enough to express a straightforward reaction—to condemn their crudity or praise their frankness— but it was somewhat more difficult to write a judicious criticism.[15] There is little to wonder at in More's perplexity. He had admitted some years before that, with few exceptions, contemporary novels struck him as so "unreal" that he could scarcely read them,[16] such periodicals as the *Dial* disgusted him,[17] and he despised the entire literary world of New York and Greenwich Village.[18]

Nevertheless, he wrote the article; in its English version it is "Modern Currents in American Literature" (*NSE*, I, 53-72). His tone throughout is condescending and sarcastic. He begins by passing over "our most accomplished novelist, Edith Wharton," "our eminent poets, Edwin Arlington Robinson and Robert Frost,"[19] and "the host of prolific penmen, extending from the fairly distinguished output of Booth Tarkington, through the respectable mediocrity of Hamlin Garland and Meredith Nicholson and their kind, down to that nadir of popular success, Harold Bell Wright." There is little to be said "about these purveyors to the market, from Mrs. Wharton to Mr. Wright, save that they are turning out books of more or less honest craftsmanship, in better or worse English, with this or that smear of local colour. We read them for entertainment, but do not talk about them a great deal" (53). There is another group of writers, less numerous than the first but more consciously modern, who attract greater attention, both critical and legal, by the audacity and salaciousness of their work. This group includes Amy Lowell, Cabell, Joseph Hergesheimer, Sinclair Lewis, Dreiser, Sherwood Anderson, and Dos Passos.

In one sense this second group is not American at all, since they derive their inspiration from a similar movement in England and beyond that in France and Russia. But in another sense they are American, for "without exception they are animated by a whole-hearted contempt for New England Puritanism and all it means" (54). Their antipathy has its origins in a number of causes: in the local pride of the Midwestern writers, in a kind of patriotism which resents the supposed English culture of New England, and especially in a rejection of religion and morality, for which the New England Puritans and their nineteenth-century descendants stand. Quite naturally the rebels desire to emancipate art from the responsibilities of life; ironically, their success in realizing this ambition is the ruination of their art.

Dividing the literary rebels into esthetes and realists, More begins his detailed treatment of them with the esthetes. Of these he finds Amy Lowell the most finished artist, but he thinks that since her best work is her more regular verse, she might better have avoided the ambitious programs to which she became attached and have contented herself with tradition. The "most talked of" esthete is James Branch Cabell, but his fame is owing chiefly to the postal authorities. About *Jurgen* More is somewhat uncertain, admiring scattered portions but finding it on the whole "superficial," "sophisticated," and "snobbish"; Cabell's other works are "trivial" (58-60). Cabell's artistic theory comes closer to More's liking because it maintains that the function of art is to embody the illusions that inspire men; but insofar as it regards good and bad as merely esthetic conventions, it subordinates ethics to esthetics, which means the death of serious emotion in literature. Joseph Hergesheimer is only questionably an esthete; for though his style is more polished than the realists', it is so affected and obscure that More hesitates to admit that he is an artist.

More credits Edgar Lee Masters with having first discovered the identifying theme of American realism, the sordidness of the Midwestern town, but he apparently regards Masters as of only historical interest. *Spoon River Anthology* was a "malodorous flash in the pan" followed by works of "unfailing dullness" (69). Sinclair Lewis is more popular, but *Main Street* is a "drab and drizzling" book (69). Sherwood Anderson, although he occasionally reveals a genuinely poetic talent, unfortunately has no restraint. At its worst, his work is the stream of consciousness gone putrid; at its best, it has too close a resemblance to the work of Gertrude Stein, "that adventuress into the lunar madnesses of literary cubism" (70). Intellectually superior to most of the writing of the other realists is the fiction of John Dos Passos, but "as a reflection of life [it] is about the lowest we have yet produced." *Manhattan Transfer*, with its "spattered filth," More likens "to an explosion in a cesspool" (63).

Of all the writers discussed in the essay, Dreiser gets fullest treatment, for it is chiefly through Dreiser that More has come to understand the origins and significance of the realists. He had earlier published a piece entitled "Theodore Dreiser, Philosopher,"[20] in which he describes Dreiser's thought as a muddle of Nietzscheism and humanitarianism. Now, drawing his information from Dreiser's *A Book About Myself*, More summarizes Dreiser's early life to show the influences that produce the typical realist: small-town Midwestern origins, an uncritical or imaginatively impoverished religion, esthetic and emotional deprivation, poor education, removal from the small town to the city, and a subsequent experience of police courts, unsavory streets, and scandal-ridden homes. No wonder, therefore, that Dreiser wrote *An American Tragedy*.[21]

It is difficult to find merit in More's essay. Some of its judgments have a certain accuracy. Dreiser is the best of the realists; Amy Lowell has held up as well as, but no better than, any of the other esthetes; and More's prophecy that in twenty years they would all be forgotten (72) has overtaken a few—although it could hardly help doing that.[22] Considering the wholesale method of his denunciation, we must see its accuracy as largely accidental. "Modern Currents in American Literature" is one of the poorest of his critical essays.

III   *The Moral Law and the Purity of Art*

The cause of this general decay in contemporary literature, both American and European, More finds in the widespread acceptance of the theory that there are no moral laws governing life, or none at least which apply to art (*NSE*, I, 72)—a point he develops in sections II and III of "The Demon of the Absolute" (*NSE*, I, 11-29). Admitting the impossibility of establishing absolute standards for the evaluation of literature and the other arts, he yet insists that history attests to a consistency of human taste so universal as to justify the conclusion "that the law of taste is the least changeable fact of human nature, less changeable than religious creeds, far less changeable than scientific theories" (12-13). Coleridge's standards for literature—and Coleridge is particularly relevant because he enjoys great favor among contemporary esthetic critics—can be reduced to four propositions. First, the value of a work of art depends on its content of truth. Second, our sense of its truth comes from our pleasure in it. Third, pleasures vary in permanence, the most permanent being the best. Fourth, pleasures vary in value and importance, according to the faculty of the mind to which they are addressed. Assuming the obviousness of the first two propositions, More argues that the greatest works of art are those which give not only the most lasting pleasures, for the animal pleasures of naturalistic art might be said to be continuously appealing, but—like the works of Homer, Virgil, Dante, and Shakespeare—a higher order of pleasure. The inverted universality of the naturalist, besides, tends to cloy; and though art may show the bestial in man, it achieves lasting significance by showing what is distinctively human.

Insofar as both estheticism and realism deny the relevance of moral criteria to art, they are both, in More's eyes, naturalistic. Thus, his criticism of naturalism applies to them equally. But in several of his essays he treats estheticism separately and at length.

The school of pure art which he discusses in his essays on Joyce and Proust and in "The Demon of the Absolute" is one whose outlines are clearer today than they were in More's own time. It begins, in the novel, with Flaubert and includes, or is said to include, some of the most characteristic work of James, Joyce, Proust, Virginia Woolf, Camus, and other twentieth-century writers. Its ideal is a novel of "pure presentation"—devoid, that is, of all authorial commentary—in which the primary value is esthetic, a novel from which all moral or social value is excluded. It is an art, as More describes it in connection with Proust, which extracts the reality of life from all associations with practical utility and convention, as a kind of pure vision of reality (not unlike, I suggest, More's own early view of religion) that is freed of any relationship or convention which interprets that reality or stands between it and the observer.

As in other schools, particular works imperfectly meet the ideal; some novels considered as belonging to the school of pure art—I think of Joyce's *Ulysses* and of Woolf's *Mrs Dalloway* —seem not to aim at quite so pure a vision of reality, whatever a pure vision of reality may be. At any rate, it is the concept, the spirit of the thing, rather than particular works with which More is concerned in "The Demon of the Absolute." This spirit he catches in a quotation from Ortega y Gasset: "To rejoice or suffer with the human lot which a work of art may incidentally suggest or present to us, is a very different thing from the true artistic pleasure. More than that: this occupation with the human element of the work is essentially incompatible with pure aesthetic fruition" (*NSE*, I, 32).

We know from More's essays on Joyce and Proust that he had some doubt about the possibility of pure fiction. *Remembrance of Things Past* is "a criticism of life as didactic as any that Matthew Arnold would demand" (*NSE*, III, 59). Despite Proust's adherence to the theory of pure art, More insists, Proust well knew that his work was didactic, for his variations on the theme of lust and perversion are an argument that life is a succession of unappeasable desires to which the only appropriate reaction is a fearful and comprehensive revulsion. So too of Joyce, whose writings show that if man cannot find value and meaning in the higher world of spiritual ideals he will find them in "that vast dark region of the soul below the plain of ordered and rationalized life" (*NSE*, III, 80). But More had two other objections to so-called pure literature: first, it leads to incomprehensibility; second, because it cuts itself off from the universal appeals that we find in the great art of the past, nothing great can come of it.

The difficulties of Camus' *The Stranger* and Joyce's *Portrait*, to take two examples of the type, tend to support More's belief. After surveying the opposing interpretations of the *Portrait* which have been put forth by reputable critics and students of Joyce, Wayne C. Booth concludes in *The Rhetoric of Fiction* that Joyce has succeeded so well in repressing judgment in the novel that the question of what the work means—of whether it is the ironic portrait of an arrogant and foolish young man or an essentially sympathetic story of the artist coming to maturity—cannot be answered by an examination of internal evidence. Which is to say that the novel—whatever its other value—does not surrender its meaning and cannot therefore be fully understood. "The creation and the enjoyment of art can never be a completely neutral activity," Booth concludes. "Though different works of art require different kinds of judgment for their enjoyment, . . . no work, not even the shortest lyric, can be written in complete moral, intellectual and aesthetic neutrality."[23]

Booth's argument, however, is not quite the same as More's. For one thing, while he does not believe that moral questions are irrelevant in the appraisal of literature, Booth contends here

not that a work of art must embody a certain moral standard but
only that, if it is to be intelligible, it must embody a standard
of some sort—moral, intellectual, or esthetic—which the reader
can infer from the work. For another, Booth is concerned with
a problem to which More gives little attention—with the adapta-
tion of technical means to intended effects. More, strangely
enough, finds no difficulty in the *Portrait;* his objections are to
the incomprehensibility of *Ulysses* and *Finnegans Wake.* Even in
them, however, he does not object to the difficulty of apprehend-
ing the author's standards, which he thinks he sees clearly enough,
but to the intricacies of the Joycean pun and the obscurities
of stream of consciousness.

In developing his other objection to pure literature—namely,
that pure fiction cuts itself off from the universal appeals we
find in the art of the past—More makes a comparison between
certain great works of the past and one real and another hypothetical or alleged work of pure art. Da Vinci's "Last Supper"
"is a truer work of art than the deftest whirl of colours ever
painted," the *Aeneid* is superior to "Kubla Kahn," Bach's "Mass
in B Minor" "is still a miracle and a rapture of sound," and all
three "are brimming with human emotion and with a brooding
sense of the eternal values of life" (*NSE,* I, 35-36). It is as
difficult to deal with such statements as it is easy to make them.
Few serious persons think Coleridge superior to Virgil or deny
the beauty of Bach's Mass; the whirl of colors is not identified.
What is significant in the comparison, however, is the program-
music standard it applies to the arts. Would the "Last Supper"
be less beautiful if we were to discover that the figures are not
Christ and the Apostles but some other group? Is it the religious
theme—which, rather than the musical theme, seems to be what
More has in mind—that determines the sublimity of Bach's Mass?
Both the painting and the Mass are brimming with emotion;
and since they have been continuously appealing, we may say
that they contain eternal—at least lasting—values. But what,
from the point of view of criticism, can be said of these values
apart from the form of the works?

Although More's discussion here is somewhat more naive than
we are entitled to expect, he is, of course, not unaware of the importance of form. Assuming the formal mastery of da Vinci,
Virgil, and Bach, he simply restricts his comments to the qualities in their works which make for greatness. And those qualities,

he believes, are rooted in profundity of theme, not in technical perfection, though some degree of technical perfection is essential to art. The simple fact is that with both the great and the not-so-great, More is virtually unconcerned with formal questions; he is always more willing to excuse technical failings in writers whose spirit he admires than to excuse moral lapses in perfectly crafted works.

While conceding, for example, that the poetry appearing in the better periodicals of the early twentieth century is artistically superior to Whittier's, he insists that Whittier's is the better because it is morally serious.[24] This judgment is another illustration of how he regards those qualities which only poetry can give—the qualities, that is, which make poetry poetry—as ancillary to moral content. There is no question but that More recognizes those qualities when he sees them, even in writers like Joyce, whom he finally condemns, but his habit is to salute them and pass on. Although he regards *Lycidas* as "the greatest short poem of any author in English, the very criterion and touchstone of poetical taste" (*NSE*, III, 190), he devotes his essay on it—an essay whose title, "How to Read *Lycidas*," might suggest a concern with the method of reading poetry and hence perhaps with poetic structure—to the attitude and expectations the reader must bring to the work.

"The essential of great tragedy," writes Roger Fry, an exponent of the esthetic criticism More disdains, is "not the emotional intensity of the events portrayed, but the vivid sense of the inevitability of their unfolding, the significance of the curve of crescendo and diminuendo which their sequence describes, together with all the myriad subsidiary evocations which, at each point, poetic language can bring in to give fullness and density to the whole organic unity."[25] More too is interested in inevitability, sequence, significance—the inevitability of moral law, the sequence of cause and effect in morality, the eternal significance of human life. Is it not possible that his moral laws work upon us in literature—at times or in part—through the curves and crescendos which Fry has in mind?

Whatever its answer, the question is not insignificant; serious students of literature might well want to ask it, and others like it, after so many centuries of predominantly moral appraisal. To More such questions are unanswerable. "If you should ask me by what rhetorical devices or by what instrument of representation one poem or one work of art appeals more successfully than another to the higher faculty within us, . . . I would reply frankly that the solution of this problem of the imagination may be beyond my powers of critical analysis" (*NSE*, I, 24). "I am not competent to explain by what devices, by what choice of words, Milton obtains his sublime effect . . . ; indeed I question whether any skill of criticism can penetrate to the heart of that mystery of the word which we call inspiration, and leave [it] at that" (*NSE*, III, 200).

More's error, therefore, is neither in saying that life is moral nor in insisting on the relationships that exist between literature and morality. It is, first, in so stressing the moral aspect of literature and in so neglecting the formal or technical as to seem to conceive of literature as a pleasurable philosophy only and, second, in being led either by his impatience with the formal experimentation of certain modern writers (Joyce and James, for example) or by his revulsion from their frank presentation of sordidness, crime, and sensuality (as in Joyce and Dostoyevski) to reject the whole of what they are doing. His rejection of much modern criticism is attributable to this error. He acknowledges in his Preface to *The Drift of Romanticism* the limits of his own method; there is no reason to suppose that he would not have acknowledged the validity of methods—though not of all methods —for which he might have had no aptitude. Convinced, however, that the most serious concerns in life are moral and philosophical and that estheticism and naturalism would not only destroy art but might also destroy civilization—the disease of the modern age "is chiefly of the imagination; we are poisoned by our poets" (*NSE*, II, 55)—he reacts strongly and unfairly against those who deny or ignore the moral basis of art. The younger critics of the 1920's, he believes, gave their attention to formal or esthetic criticism simply because they neither had nor could conceive of a serious view of life.[26]

Unfortunately, while vituperating estheticism and realism, More does little for his own position but assert it—and too frequently in language which seems to imply a belief that the poet works by a process of mystification at which the critic is obliged to connive and that to attempt to analyze the process is to subject poetry to the same illicit probing of reason which works havoc in religion and philosophy. *The Study of English Literature* describes the effect of poetry as "something which

for lack of a better term we may call mystical elevation" (179);
the language of the *New Shelburne Essays* is often equally
hierophantic. The true artist

> is one who, by the subtle, insinuating power of the imagination,
> by just appreciation of the higher emotions as well as the lower,
> by the revelation of a sad sincerity, shall I call it, in his own
> soul, gives us always to feel that the true universal in human
> nature, the faculty by which man resembles man as a being
> different from the beast, is that part of him that is "noble
> in reason," the master and not the slave of passion. True art is
> thus humanistic rather than naturalistic; and its gift of high
> and permanent pleasure is the response of our own breast to the
> artist's delicately revealed sense of that divine control, moving
> like the spirit of God upon the face of the waters. (*NSE*, I, 24)

But criticism—ours as well as More's—requires discrimination;
we should not be deceived as to the true direction or value of
his theories by the accidental coloring they are given in
polemics, certainly not by the expression they receive from a
man by this time, as I hope to show, grown weary—and therefore
impatient—of restating truths he takes to be both obvious and
as old as Plato. More's criteria have their limits at best, but
they are not displayed at their best in most of the *New Shelburne
Essays*. Still, the conception of literature he holds at this time
is essentially the one he had always held; it is better expressed
elsewhere in his writings.

His first serious interest in literature followed his youthful
disappointment in materialism and rationalism, which drove him
to "biography and letters" in the hope of discovering in them "the
secret of existence" (*Oxford Diary*, sec. V). He loved it therefore for its presentation of truths which he believed could only
be expressed in symbol and allegory; yet those truths were always
religious ones. His preference for Homer over Shakespeare, for
example, rests on the assumption that the function of literature
is not only to depict human passion and the variety and depth of
human experience but to bring religious peace.[27] Finally, when
More had found that peace, but in Platonism and Christianity
rather than in literature, he tended to value most those writers
and books which confirmed his moral and religious convictions.
Literature might have a different value for others; but so far as
it possessed truth and beauty it could only point in one direction:

Not every man's thoughts and visions and desires, as by them he would remould the gross material of experience, are capable of passing into enduring literature, but rather those which conform with actual truths, visualizing a beauty finer than that comprehended by the seeing eye, grasping a law of justice more infallible than the tangled events of this earth ever obey, conveying a significance beyond any evaluation of the senses. By such distinctions I lay hold of a strange philosophy which tells me that the soul's assurance of truth is not a dream evoked arbitrarily by any man's imagination, but an intuition more or less perfectly grasped of veritable realities. These books on which I depend for most of my noetic life are effective just as they are a history of what has been known of these realities by other souls in the past and set down for the recreation of any who can spell out the record. So do they charm into peace because they lure us to the belief that some time, if not here and now, our soul may be lifted to that world of immutable Ideas which lie in all their splendour before the eye of Plato's God.

In this way all worthy art and literature, all genuine philosophy, are a mystical initiation. . . .[28]

IV *The New Humanism*

Throughout the first three decades of the century Irving Babbitt and Paul Elmer More had been attracting a number of disciples and supporters who, despite their differences, were sufficiently united in principles and general aims to be known by and to acknowledge a common designation. These were the New Humanists of the 1920's and 1930's.[29]

Babbitt's influence came principally from his teaching at Harvard; More's from his editorship of the *Nation* and from his writings, although to some extent from his teaching too. Their three-decade denunciation of modernism had also provoked antagonism, both from the naturalists and from others who for various reasons found the humanism of Babbitt and More an inadequate measure of literature and society. By the late 1920's a widespread controversy had come into being, mainly in the pages of literary journals, between the New Humanists and their opponents. The chief organs of the Humanists were the *Bookman,* its successor the *American Review,* and the *Forum;* many of More's later essays appeared in these magazines. The anti-Humanists, comprising a variety of parties, had a wider selection of journals, of which the *New Republic* is the most important.

Hound and Horn, the *Sewanee Review,* the *Saturday Review of Literature,* and in England the *Criterion* all took part in the dispute, though not so wholeheartedly on one side. The quarrel has been nicely crystallized in two books which appeared in 1930—Norman Foerster's collection of Humanist essays, *Humanism and America,* and another collection, *The Critique of Humanism,* which C. Hartley Grattan brought out in reply.[30]

Primarily the work of the younger Humanists, *Humanism and America* is an indirect tribute to Babbitt and More; there is nothing in it which is not at least implicit in their writings. The younger contributors, however, have their own emphasis and tone; those writing on contemporary literature, for instance, are less sweeping and severe in their condemnations than More. Some of the essays are general statements of Humanist principles; others are more specifically concerned with science, religion, education, art, and literature. That the Humanists are only a loosely knit group, something of a coalition perhaps, can be seen from the facts that one of them, T. S. Eliot, is regarded suspiciously by some of the others[31] and that another, Bernard Bandler II, would also contribute an attack upon More to *The Critique of Humanism.*

Humanism and America opens with Foerster's Preface, which is followed by five pieces on miscellaneous topics: "The Pretensions of Science" by More's brother Louis T. More; Babbitt's "Humanism: An Essay at Definition"; More's contribution, "The Humility of Common Sense," a reprinting of sections IV and V of "The Demon of the Absolute"; George R. Elliott's "The Pride of Modernity"; and T. S. Eliot's short piece, "Religion Without Humanism." Admitting that humanism offers neither the intellectual discipline of science or philosophy nor—what the modern world needs most—the emotional discipline of religion, Eliot argues that these activities lose their sanity if they are not imbued with humanism; without it, science becomes a mere process of technical research occasionally erupting "into sentimental monstrosities like the Life Force, or Professor Whitehead's God" and religion becomes "either a sentimental tune, or an emotional debauch; or in theology, a skeleton dance of fleshless dogmas, or in ecclesiasticism, a soulless political club" (111).

The next six essays are on the arts: Frank Jewett Mather's "The Plight of Our Arts," Alan Reynolds Thompson's "The Dilemma of Modern Tragedy," Robert Shafer's "An American

Tragedy," Harry Hayden Clark's "Pandora's Box in American Fiction," Stanley P. Chase's "Dionysus in Dismay," and Gorham B. Munson's "Our Critical Spokesmen." While all of these writers stress the failings of contemporary literature and art, some are inclined to blame society as much as the artist and to see the function of humanism as that of raising the spiritual and esthetic level of society. Mather attributes the condition of contemporary art to the vulgarity of an industrial, democratic society. Thompson ascribes the dilemma of modern tragedy to man's no longer believing in either heroism or will. Somewhat sophistically, Shafer finds in Dreiser's *An American Tragedy* an inherent defect of the naturalistic novel which, since its fundamental theme is the insignificance of human life, inevitably defeats itself— that is, becomes insignificant—in proportion as its succeeds. Viewing the failure of American novelists of the nineteenth as well as the twentieth century to produce any great work under the inspiration of their common themes, Clark suggests that they turn instead to the "soul's conflict between appetite and aspiration on its quest for an exalted inward happiness" (203). Chase considers and exaggerates the obscurity of modern poetry. And Gorham B. Munson calls the movement led by Babbitt and More the only critical movement of international significance in America; the rest of American criticism, from 1915 to 1930, is "a tragi-comedy, almost a tragi-farce" (232).

Three essays on more general subjects round out the book. "Behaviour and Continuity," by Bernard Bandler II, discusses the irrelevance of experimental psychology to humanist ethics. Sherlock B. Gass, in "The Well of Discipline," affirms the superiority of literature to physical science as the basic educational discipline. Originally an undergraduate commencement address, Richard Lindley Brown's "Courage and Education" attributes the decline in value of the study of literature in American colleges to the facile dilettantism of the elective system and the increasing emphasis given modern literature at the expense of the classics.

Like *Humanism and America*, *The Critique of Humanism* is also a tribute to Babbitt and More, though ironically so, for it was provoked, we are told in an Editor's Note, by "the return to a more central position in American criticism of the New Humanists, the disciples of Irving Babbitt and Paul Elmer More." Despite the fact that its contributors represent a wider variety of positions than the Humanists, their criticisms are not particularly varied. They make much of an alleged lack of decorum, moderation, and common sense among the Humanists, particularly in Babbitt and More; and they object to the identification of humanism with "a small clique of the self-anointed," as Henry Hazlitt puts it, who "arrogated to themselves a name that stood, in the fifteenth century, for a genuinely liberating attitude, and degraded it to . . . a rationalization of neophobia and a piece of special pleading for the genteel tradition" (96).

The Humanists' inability to find value in contemporary literature and culture is ascribed to a failure of understanding. Because they cannot understand their society, writes R. P. Blackmur, they deal with it only as censors and suppressors, measuring it by a foreign tradition constructed out of elements of dead cultures. According to Malcolm Cowley, Humanism is only a collection of conservative, snobbish, theological, and puritanical attitudes and beliefs which can never humanize society. Several contributors point out that, with the single exception of T. S. Eliot, there is not one writer in Foerster's volume who has any standing as an artist. All in all, the *Critique* ranges from a mere tweaking of the noses of Babbitt and More to cogent analyses of essential defects in their position. Besides Blackmur and Cowley, the contributors who are best known today are Edmund Wilson, Allen Tate, Kenneth Burke, Yvor Winters, and Lewis Mumford.

The essays by Winters and Tate are particularly relevant to Paul Elmer More: the first, as a comment on his reading of contemporary literature; the second, as a criticism of his conception of tradition. In "Poetry, Morality, and Criticism," Winters argues that the Humanists are concerned with the morality of the actions and reasonings embodied in poetic subjects rather than with the writing itself and that they stress the correctness of paraphrased doctrine rather than that of poetic expressions, the non-paraphrasable aspect of poetic language. He also points out—naming Allen Tate, Hart Crane, Elizabeth Madox Roberts, Katherine Anne Porter, and Glenway Wescott—that there are a number of young American writers, uncorrupted by either "mid-Americanism" or "Menckenism," who are in the line of the great poetic stylists but whom the Humanists—even Paul Elmer More, "incomparably the best of them" (324)—have shown themselves incapable of treating.

The most valuable essay in the book is Allen Tate's "The

Fallacy of Humanism," which, although some of its criticisms appear elsewhere in the volume too, is the most thorough and coherent exposition of the central defect of More's Humanism: its conception of tradition. According to Tate, the Humanists go to literature in search of a philosophy which is both explicit and more satisfying than any they can find elsewhere in a purer or non-literary form. They look upon literature, that is, as a surrogate for a philosophy and a church; the extravagance of this expectation produces their quarrel with it. Philosophical particles, so to speak, can be found here and there in the literature of the past; from these the Humanists collect a tradition to which they expect modern man and modern literature to conform.

The fallacy of their procedure is that it is a circular reasoning, a continual begging of the question, for they have no historical or philosophical authority for what they select. While they claim to select from the past with the authority of the past, that authority exists nowhere but in their own minds. As with More, the authority of the past is an "infinite regression" (145), an appeal from any historical moment to the authority of a past further back: "If the ethical imagination *is* imagination it must deal with images; but the Humanists give us only a digest of ancient cultures; they leave to abstract inference a conception of the particular culture in which the humane life may be lived" (140).

Obviously, Tate's criticism does not apply to More in all details; More did find philosophy in a purer form in Plato. Yet, while More was particularly offended by the whole tone of Tate's essay, which he termed an "ignorant and conceited outburst" (*NSE*, III, 14), he admitted that much of what Tate said was right—that Humanism was not self-sufficient but needed a more certain, a religious and historical authority to sustain it.[32] But Tate's criticism applies not only to what might be called More's pre-Christian humanism; it applies to *The Greek Tradition* and to the literary tradition of the *Shelburne Essays*. Although More acknowledges the necessity of an authoritative Church and confesses his belief in an historical revelation, he interprets Christianity as a religion of one essential dogma. And he makes that reduction in the interests of orthodoxy and in opposition to Protestant individualism. For all his insistence on the conservative imagination, More never surrenders himself to what comes down from the past.

But there is no point in oversimplifying. Every intelligent and responsible being must rely on his own understanding and conscience; a tradition, however it is formed, is known by a mind or a consensus. More's beliefs, of whatever kind, are a mixture of traditionalism and individualism. But while in politics he inclines to the side of conservatism, in religion his individualism is stronger, whether he identifies himself with a particular Church or not. The reason is probably that the noetic and moral life was primary for him and the life of affairs only second, that stability in the second guaranteed freedom in the first. Since stability, order, and continuity in society had an intimate and certain relationship with institutions now in being, it was better to preserve those institutions with their imperfections than to risk a general unsettling of life through changes prompted by theory. Property secure, men—some men, anyway—could in some degree of safety (though life was uncertain under any conditions) give themselves to the good life; property insecure, who knew the result? More's conservatism, therefore, while it was rooted in conceptions of justice, loyalty, and humility, was also practical— the *most prudent* attitude toward the material life.

In the same way perhaps, his religion in its late phase was conservative; he defends traditional and institutional forms— the Church and its creeds, sacraments, and ritual. But he reveres these only as the external shapes and protectors, as he might say, of essential religion. He understands no creed as a Church body might insist that it be understood; he defends sacramentalism, but he interprets the sacraments in a private sense which may or may not correspond to anyone else's interpretation. The noetic life as he knows and practices it is the seeking out of truths which can be known in their fullest—that is, can only be known—to each man individually. Recognizing that men have common needs and a common nature, he examines the records of human experience and compares that experience with his own.

But, as I have said before, More takes from it what satisfies his own needs. Which is to say that he interprets or defines tradition by his personal needs and understanding, in the belief that the only meaning it can have for him is that which he understands it to have. He is never so traditional or so humble as to subordinate his judgment in the most important matters to any judgment, historical or corporate, which runs counter to it. He respects orthodoxy, defends it, perhaps hankers after it; but his conception of what it is has little that is orthodox in any meaningful sense. Thus, while he never compromises his sincerity or his integrity, and while as the term "Christianity" is used it is large enough to encompass his beliefs, he has defined Christianity by denying, in the interests of his psychological dualism, a tremendous amount of what the Christian Churches have held to be *there*. Even what he keeps—the "one essential doctrine"— he understands in a private sense.

The same may be said of his conception of English literature. He is not to be tested here by fidelity to a historical revelation or an institutional authority; there is no orthodoxy in literary history or criticism. But we may say at least that More takes little account of some of the most striking and characteristic accomplishments of English literature.

From the point of view of subsequent or at least of present fame—to come back to the Humanist controversy of the 1920's and 1930's—the anti-Humanists must be awarded the victory. Certainly Wilson, Blackmur, Tate, Cowley, Burke, Mumford, and Winters are better known today than any of the Humanists except that doubtful member T. S. Eliot. This circumstance is partly attributable to the fact that Babbitt and More have been dead a quarter of a century and more, during which time their opponents have continued to live and to write. But the younger Humanists, who continued to write into the succeeding decades, have not fared quite so well as their critical antagonists. More's defense is implicit in the essay "Criticism": in the long run, civilization is the monument of the conservative critic. But is it any less the monument of the opposite kind? What killed Humanism—rather, what let it die—was not the assault of its enemies, but the Great Depression, which distracted so much of the attention of both the general public—if the general public was ever interested—and its writers from literature to politics and economics, which for a while rather discredited anything conservative, and which gave as great a boost to pragmatism and experiment as they have ever been given in this country. Still, the New Humanism was not strong enough to withstand the shock because, despite its affirmation of the spiritual uniqueness of man, it could not—as its critics constantly repeated— stimulate a vital literature.[33] Daniel Aaron refers to "a letter to the *New Republic* demanding to know the name of 'a contemporary work of art either produced by an American humanist or encouraged and approved by one.' "[34] The New Humanism's failure to enlist the artist accounts for its failure to work any lasting effect in American literature. Artists, and in the long run society, are more inspired by artists than by critics.

V More and the Humanists

Despite More's certainty that his own early work had been the only worthwhile criticism being written in England and America in the opening years of the century, he was convinced that he had suffered from not having had "the right kind of friction and emulation." He therefore found it "a thrilling experience" to watch the appearance of the younger Humanists of the 1920's,[35] who certainly had friction enough and for whom he was so largely responsible. Their work, he believed, was "altogether the most original and aggressive" criticism being done in America or England and the equal of anything being done in France (*NSE*, I, 73). Nevertheless, he was somewhat uneasy about his part in *Humanism and America*. Thinking that the volume would be more effective if it were entirely the work of the younger men,[36] who would then be free both to judge their progenitors and to modify humanist principles to meet the needs of the times, he at first intended not to contribute.[37] But there was more to his hesitancy than that. "Sometimes I get a little tired of the chatter going on about humanism, etc.," he wrote, "but the eagerness of these youngsters is on the whole amusing, and perhaps significant. At any rate we have to go on playing the game."[38] In this ambivalent frame of mind, a mixed feeling of paternal responsibility and weariness, he allowed himself to be persuaded to contribute. In the same mood he reviewed the book.

"A Revival of Humanism"[39] is More's summary of the essentials of humanism and a discussion of the importance to humanism of religion. The central beliefs of the humanist are that there is some element in man which distinguishes him from the beast, that man has free will to direct his actions and is therefore morally accountable for them, that the dualism of consciousness is as certainly known by observation and self-knowledge as any other fact of experience, and that the best preservative of morality and artistic creativity is tradition. Relying both on what the Humanists have written and on his personal acquaintance with them, he divides them into three groups according to their attitude toward religion. Some think that religion is anti-humanistic and are consequently hostile to it; some are well disposed toward it but empty it of any content; some regard a vital and doctrinal religion as an essential for a full human life. All three groups, More admits, are truly humanist; but he believes himself that only through an alliance with a doctrinal and vital religion can humanism sustain itself.

More had intended no betrayal of his associates, but Robert Shafer, for one, thought that he had conceded too much to the critics of Humanism, and particularly to Allen Tate. More denied that he had, but in his answer there is a suggestion of how little enthusiasm he had for the Humanist controversy. "Personally," he writes, "I should prefer to fight for sanity, decency, truth, rather than for a word to which after all we have no exclusive claims."[40] This attitude is a counterpart to his increasing absorption in religion, and it matches his lessening interest in literature. There are thirteen major volumes which he published after leaving the *Nation*: the last three volumes of *Shelburne Essays*, six volumes on Greek philosophy and Patristic theology, three volumes of *New Shelburne Essays* and *Pages from an Oxford Diary*. Only five of these, the last three volumes of *Shelburne Essays* and the first and third volumes of *New Shelburne Essays*, are predominantly on non-philosophical or non-religious subjects, but even they contain essays considerably older than the time of their publication. The essay on George Borrow in *The Demon of the Absolute* dates from 1912; although the last volume of *Shelburne Essays* appeared in 1921, nearly everything contained in it had been written by 1918.

Thus, the last two decades of More's life were given over principally to philosophical, Patristic, and other religious studies. He wrote in 1921, on his fifty-seventh birthday, that he was "just beginning the work I have been preparing for all my life."[41] That work, of course, was *The Greek Tradition;* by the end of the decade it was so absorbing his interest that literature was virtually a distraction. In 1929 he recalled a time when he could pick up any book with a sense of expectancy; that sense had now disappeared.[42] The Humanist controversy prompted him to remark "that we may all be taking literature a little too seriously. We must not forget that when all is said, art is the adornment and not the substance of life."[43] By 1931 he had concluded that "theology is the only interesting topic after all,"[44] and he complained as he was leaving to take an LL.D. from the University of Glasgow, "Hang it all! I have a trunk full of doctoral hoods, but no one will give me the only thing I covet, a D.D."[45]

The enthusiasm of such late literary essays as those on Trollope (*NSE*, I, 89-125) and Milton (*NSE*, III, 184-202) hardly refutes the conjecture that religion was becoming his chief preoccupation. The piece on Trollope was his payment of a "deep debt of gratitude"[46] to an author with whom he had shared a kind of companionship; he was inspired to write on Milton by the thrill he had taken from reading that poet after having passed "through the valley of the shadow of death" (*NSE*, III, 184). Reading Milton, for that matter, had always been an experience like the reading of the Scriptures. When in *The Christ of the New Testament* he reconstructs the life of Christ, More imagines Him speaking now in the words of the gospels, now in the words of *Paradise Regained* (57).

For Paul Elmer More literature had always been ancillary to philosophy. It became now ancillary to religion, and thus became less important to him than it was during the years when he read it for symbolic renderings of truths which he believed theology and creed only distorted. "My mind has been of recent years, and still is," he wrote a few years before his death, "so engaged in certain philosophical and religious problems that it has taken a violent effort of the will to keep my attention on a literary subject and to get out any ideas. But I do hope to come back to literature some day."[47] He never did come back, however, with anything like the wholehearted attention and enthusiasm which he had given to it during the years of his writing of the *Shelburne Essays*.

CHAPTER 6

Conclusion

THE GREATEST of More's works, in T. S. Eliot's opinion, is *The Greek Tradition*.[1] It is, beyond doubt, the best manifestation in More's writings of "the concentrated mind seeking God"; his most sustained and single-minded study, it is also the most perfect fruit of the life of scholarship as he conceived that life, "of an intellectual purpose steadily followed year after year, binding day to day in orderly interest."[2] Objections to be made against it on grounds of historical accuracy are rendered largely irrelevant by the fact that despite its freight of historical detail it is essentially a philosophical endeavor—an invitation to the moral life and a protest against philosophical naturalism. For sustained personal intensity, for controlled handling of a wealth of material, for its demonstration of the mind's ability through persistent search to find purpose in life, and above all for its revelation of the moral and intellectual integrity of the writer, *The Greek Tradition* is indeed More's greatest work. My one reservation is that the idiosyncratic conclusions of the later volumes, and to a lesser extent of the whole, tend to limit its value to that of example only.

The *Shelburne Essays*, despite their being part of the same personal inquiry as *The Greek Tradition* and despite their being imbued with More's particular form of dualism, are much less idiosyncratic in their judgments on writers, works, and events; they are therefore more serviceable to the student of literature than *The Greek Tradition* is to the student of religion. Their effectiveness as example is somewhat reduced by their diffusion of subject matter and point of view, but they manifest to some degree all the virtues of *The Greek Tradition;* because they have an even greater range, they are a better illustration of their author's erudition and of the philosophical quality of his mind.

There is little profit, however, in drawing out these distinctions; what is true of the one work is true *mutatis mutandis* of the other.

Perhaps the highest praise to be given the *Shelburne Essays,* taking the essays either separately or together, is that they exemplify the ideal of humanistic education More describes in "Academic Leadership"—"a disciplining of the higher faculty of the imagination to the end that the student may behold, as it were in one sublime vision, the whole scale of being in its range from the lowest to the highest under the divine decree of order and subordination, without losing sight of the immutable veracity at the heart of all development . . ." (*SE,* IX, 56). Whether in literature or in philosophy, More judges writers— even nations and societies—according to the firmness of their apprehension of those ideals and moral laws which have been central in Western thought since the times of Socrates and Christ—ideals and laws which he knows by introspection as well as by the study of texts. It is an easier thing to acquire the technical apparatus of modern criticism and research than it is to acquire the habit of seeing the whole of life philosophically, as More has done. There are few other modern critics about whom it can be so truly said that to read their works constitutes in itself a liberal education.

Stuart P. Sherman, one-time disciple of Babbitt and More, accused More of writing too exclusively for the cultivated and the learned.[3] On occasion we find apparent corroboration of the charge in More's own words, as when he writes to William Roscoe Thayer, "I find myself excluding the general reader from my mind and writing with the expected judgment of yourself and two or three other men quite distinctly before me."[4] But while the remark is disdainful of the general reader, it is more accurately appreciated as an expression of More's concern for the quality of his work.

As a matter of fact, More was quite interested in the general reader—not as the term might be taken to indicate the entire market for printed matter, but as it indicates the reader who is seriously interested in literature, philosophy, and history but who has no specialized training in those studies. He preferred editorial practices, for example, which brought an older work within reach of contemporary readers to those which treated it as a scholarly text—a preference not always approved by literary scholars.[5] Yet More was no mere popularizer of other men's ideas. His studies of Plato are not a digest of Platonism but a practice of it; his literary studies are introductions to the literary work, not substitutes for it. In education he held the same balanced ideal of intellectual seriousness without pedantic specialization. He complained "that Kittredge, the great English scholar, had reduced the teaching of literature to a killing pedantry, that Moore taught the history of religions without, so far as one can see, a spark of religion in his soul, that Pound at the head of the Law School was undermining the very principle of law, and that only Babbitt had a true message for the hungry student."[6]

There was a time, long before More acquired his late reverence for the incarnate Word, when he saw in the Logos of Greek and Gnostic doctrine a conception which could fittingly be applied to literature (*SE*, VII, 239). This respect for the word animates his criticism, which, except for his essays on twentieth-century literature, is always primarily appreciative. It enhances the work it considers; it never suggests, by its tone or its manner, that it is more worthy of interest than its subject. So far as he can, More enters into the work in the belief that in literature the significance of life is most clearly and profoundly seen. Never concerned with merely observing, "by scrupulous limitation of invoked feeling, what is actually *there*," or with making of the work simply "the point of convergence of known and discerned purpose," he would experience the work within himself. No "neutral, precise echo" of an external object, he would feel within himself what has inspired the artist,[7] knowing all the time that the work is superior to the moment that produced it. Viewing the process whereby the raw experience of life becomes transmuted through literature into a significant design and seeing in it how literature becomes an analogue of the ideal world out of which the practical world arises and into which it is forever passing, More concludes that "literature may not too presumptuously be cherished as the final end of existence" (*SE*, VII, 239). The claim may sound pretentious, but it helps explain the earnestness—one of the great virtues—of the *Shelburne Essays*.

Another of the more valuable things in More's writings is the frequent sally into literary or intellectual history in which he takes some idea, tendency, or form and traces it back to its origins or forward to the present moment. Even brief, passing references, like a speculation on the origin of the idea of the noble savage (*SE*, X, 93-95), can be provocative; the wide-ranging inquiries—either in single essays or running through a number of essays or books—into romanticism, deism, natural law, religious dualism, or the character of a national literature are especially valuable. One of the last is the history of American literature which is scattered through the *Shelburne Essays* and his uncollected writings.

The distinctive marks of American literature, he believed, are traceable to the cultural privations and religious excesses of New England Puritanism. The emphasis on sin and morality and the morbid sense of isolation to which these privations and excesses gave rise are evident enough in the literature of the Puritans; they also determine the themes and the tone of much of the later literature and some of the other peculiarities of American culture. After a period of secularization in the colonial era, they appear first in Philip Freneau and Charles Brockden Brown, next in Irving and Bryant, and then in the major writers of the nineteenth century. The isolation and morbidity find expression in Hawthorne and Poe; the sense of sin, in Hawthorne; and the morality, in Emerson, Thoreau, Longfellow, and Whittier. Hawthorne's quietude and feeling of isolation descend to Mary Wilkins Freeman and Sarah Orne Jewett, although the same traits are to be found in the fiction of Longfellow, Whittier, Holmes, and Donald G. Mitchell. Emerson's influence comes down to Whitman, William James, Mary Baker Eddy, and the broad humanitarianism of the end of the century. The homely tradition of Longfellow and Whittier finds its last expression in Mitchell; Charles Eliot Norton and Henry Adams inherit the Puritan sense of character, now thoroughly secularized; and with Adams that character ends in nihilism. In the meantime Poe's amoral virtuosity has reached the twentieth century by way of French symbolism, of which Whitman and Henry James are also antecedents; and symbolism joins with two other importations, naturalism and evolutionary science, to produce the art of the twentieth century.[8]

More was not the first to come upon all the events of this "history,"[9] and there are a few obvious gaps in it, such as the absence of Cooper, Twain, and Melville. Cooper, however, is less likely to be missed today than he once might have been;

Twain's leveling irreverence would hardly have attracted More; and, although there was nothing to prevent More's writing on Melville, revival of interest in Melville did not begin until after the completion of the *Shelburne Essays.* But rather than claim too much for More's conception of American literature and have to apologize for omissions, I concede that it is largely a history of the rise and decline of New England literature, which More seems to have regarded as pretty much the only literature we have. Taken that way, More's conception of the American literary tradition may still have its shortcomings, as in its reliance on an older conception of Hawthorne which exaggerated his isolation and morbidity; and it may still contain an occasional judgment which later opinion would correct, as in the view that, except for the vitality of his experience, Thoreau was only a lesser Emerson (*SE,* V, 109, 128). But such shortcomings, minor at most, are compensated for, as in More's discovery that virtually the whole of German romanticism is explicitly or implicitly contained in Thoreau's journals and formal writings.[10] Considering the fact that More had practically completed it by 1920, before the flourishing of interest in American literature as a separate study and before the long line of historical and critical works on American literature which began appearing in the 1920's, More's is a respectable historical construction.

On a number of points, his work anticipates conclusions or discoveries of later scholars. The fiction of Sarah Orne Jewett, Mary Wilkins Freeman, and other New England regionalists, writes Carl Van Doren, presents "quaint interiors scrupulously described; rounds of minute activity familiarly portrayed; skimpy moods analyzed with a delicate competence of touch; . . . the atrophy of the emotions which . . . often grows upon the celibate."[11] Commenting earlier on the same writers, More observes: "States of mind they can describe; the conscience of an individual or of a people they can analyze; characters petrified into some tragic or exquisitely pathetic or tender reminiscence they can make real; an aspect of nature they can portray as delicately as the human mood of which it seems a shadow; but in passion or action they have almost always failed. . . . Always we have the idyllic beauty of a scene that is petrified into motionlessness, and human moods in which the active passions remain as an echo from a remote distance."[12]

Harry Levin, in *The Power of Blackness,*[13] finds that Haw-

thorne objectified and exorcized the darkness of his Puritan inheritance—which, with his solitude, was the source of his art—by
transferring it to the plane of the imagination (39) and that the
difference between Hawthorne and Poe is that Hawthorne is
concerned with "the ethics of guilt" and Poe with "the psychology
of crime" (146). More had earlier described Hawthorne's role in
"the change from the old supernaturalism" or from the "overwhelming superstition" of the old religion to "the shadowy symbolism of literature" (*SE*, I, 64-65) and distinguished between
Hawthorne's concern with moral evil and Poe's "analysis of the
sensations connected with crime" (*NSE*, I, 79).

Not only in particular judgments does More anticipate later
scholarship; his central conception that the most significant strain
in American letters is the strain of darkness, morbidity, and
preoccupation with evil which descends in one way or another
from the experiences of the New England colonists has lately
attained a new currency. Robert E. Spiller finds in the aftermath
of the Great Awakening preached by Jonathan Edwards a "tragic
realization which was repeated in the work of Poe, Hawthorne,
and Melville; O'Neill, Eliot, and Faulkner."[14] The centrality
in our literature of the same tragic element is the subject of
Randall Stewart's *American Literature and Christian Doctrine*.[15]

More is no longer so unique a figure in American criticism as
he was when Mencken grudgingly called him our "nearest approach to a genuine scholar."[16] Since then there have been a
number of first-rate critics who have perfected a kind of
criticism in which More had neither interest nor, possibly, skill.
He is no longer so influential a figure as he was when he and
Babbitt deflated for a time the Romantic Movement.[17] Considering the limitations of More's standards, it is just as well that
he is not. But if it is true that "the old assumption...that esthetics
depends upon ethics," as Harry Levin says, "would not be
seriously challenged today,"[18] perhaps an interest in More's work
will revive. The *Shelburne Essays* deserve a more general esteem
than they now enjoy. Despite their being "often warped to
their respective theses," Robert E. Spiller writes, they "nevertheless are the most ambitious and often the most penetrating body
of judicial literary criticism in our literature."[19]

Notes and References

Preface

1. Paul Elmer More to Prosser Hall Frye, December 29, 1922.
2. H. L. Mencken, *Prejudices, Third Series* (New York, 1922), p. 178.
3. Paul Shorey, in a review of More's *Platonism, Nation,* CVI (February 21, 1918), 209. The review is anonymous, as are many other items, both by More and by others, which I cite without noting the anonymity. In all such instances my authority for the identity of the author is either Arthur Hazard Dakin, *A Paul Elmer More Miscellany* (Portland, Me., 1950) or the Bibliographic Note in the same author's *Paul Elmer More* (Princeton, 1960), p. 388.
4. I use the following editions of *Shelburne Essays* and *New Shelburne Essays: Shelburne Essays, First Series* (Boston and New York, 1904); *Shelburne Essays, Second Series* (Boston and New York, 1905); *Shelburne Essays, Third Series* (Boston and New York, 1905); *Shelburne Essays, Fourth Series* (Boston and New York, 1906); *Shelburne Essays, Fifth Series* (New York and London, 1908); *Shelburne Essays, Sixth Series: Studies of Religious Dualism* (Boston and New York, 1909); *Shelburne Essays, Seventh Series* (Boston and New York, 1910); *The Drift of Romanticism: Shelburne Essays, Eighth Series* (Boston and New York, 1913); *Aristocracy and Justice: Shelburne Essays, Ninth Series* (Boston and New York, 1915); *With the Wits: Shelburne Essays, Tenth Series* (Boston and New York, 1919); *A New England Group and Others: Shelburne Essays, Eleventh Series* (Boston and New York, 1921); *The Demon of the Absolute, New Shelburne Essays,* Vol. I (Princeton, 1928); *The Sceptical Approach to Religion, New Shelburne Essays,* Vol. II (Princeton, 1934); *On Being Human, New Shelburne Essays,* Vol. III (Princeton, 1936). Hereafter I cite these volumes parenthetically in the text, using the abbreviations *SE,* I, *SE,* II, etc., followed by page numbers for *Shelburne Essays,* even when the volumes have individual titles; and *NSE,* I, etc., followed by page numbers for *New Shelburne Essays.*
5. H. L. Mencken, *Prejudices, Fourth Series* (New York, 1924), p. 28.
6. PEM to Alan Reynolds Thompson, November 22, 1931.
7. Dakin, *Paul Elmer More,* pp. 275, 324.

Chapter One

1. New Haven, 1935.
2. "Marginalia, Part I," *American Review,* VIII (November 1936), 1-30, quotation, p. 2. *Pages from an Oxford Diary* (Princeton, 1937).

The Great Refusal: Being Letters of a Dreamer in Gotham (Boston and New York, 1894). *The Jessica Letters: An Editor's Romance* (New York and London, 1904).

3. PEM to Robert Shafer, October 22, 1931. Dakin thinks that More's discovery of Baur might have occurred somewhat later than the date More gives. *Paul Elmer More*, p. 44.

4. See Dakin, *Paul Elmer More*, pp. 16-19.

5. PEM to Alice More, December 16, 1888.

6. PEM to Enoch Anson More, Jr., February 7, 1889.

7. PEM to Alice More, postmarked December 21, 1914. See also PEM to Stuart P. Sherman, March 1, 1915.

8. PEM to Alice More, November 27, 1914.

9. PEM to Irving Babbitt, May 3, 1913.

10. *The Christ of the New Testament* (Princeton, 1924), pp. 198-99.

11. The statement appears in three places in More's writings: *Hellenistic Philosophies* (Princeton, 1923), p. 385; *NSE* II, 89; *Pages from an Oxford Diary*, sec. XXXII (the pages in this book are not numbered).

12. *Pages from an Oxford Diary*, secs. V and XVII.

13. PEM to Irving Babbitt, November 27, 1925. For More's treatment of Manicheism see his article, "The Influences of Hindu Thought on Manicheism," *Proceedings of the American Oriental Society*, April 1893, pp. xx-xxv.

14. See especially sec. XXVIII. In sec. XXII More distinguishes this God who faces the dark Necessity from Plato's God and from the corresponding figure in the mythology of the Gnostics.

15. PEM to Enoch Anson More, Jr. (probably May or June, 1894). The probable dates of all undated letters have been given me by Mr. A. H. Dakin.

16. The autobiographical value of *The Great Refusal* is discussed in Dakin, *Paul Elmer More*, pp. 37-43.

17. For Indian philosophy in general see Surendranath Dasgupta, *A History of Indian Philosophy*, 5 vols. (Cambridge, Eng., 1922-1955); Paul Deussen, *The Philosophy of the Upanishads*, trans. A. S. Geden (Edinburgh, 1906); Heinrich Zimmer, *Philosophies of India*, ed. Joseph Campbell, Bollingen Series, XXVI (New York, 1951). For Vedanta see Paul Deussen, *The System of the Vedanta*, trans. C. Johnson (Chicago, 1912), and Richard Garbe, "Vedanta," *Encyclopaedia of Religion and Ethics*, ed. James Hastings, XII (1928), 597-98.

18. *A Century of Indian Epigrams: Chiefly from the Sanskrit of Bhartrihari* (Boston, 1898), p. 13.

19. "Delphi and Greek Literature" originally appeared as "Two Famous Maxims of Greece," *New World*, VII (March, 1898), 18-35; "Nemesis, or the Divine Envy" also appeared in the *New World*,

VIII (December, 1899), 800-8. "Socrates" was originally the introduction to More's pamphlet *The Judgment of Socrates: Being a Translation of Plato's Apology, Crito, and the Closing Scene of Phaedo,* Riverside Literature Series, No. 129 (Boston, 1898), but those parts of it which are relevant here were not included in that publication.

20. PEM to Alice More, March 12, 1894.

21. See, e.g., PEM to Irving Babbitt, September 14, 1917, and "Irving Babbitt," *NSE,* III, 26-33.

22. PEM to Alice More, August 20, 1918.

23. PEM to Robert Shafer, October 22, 1931.

24. See William D. Geoghegan, *Platonism in Recent Religious Thought* (New York, 1958), pp. 42-55, and Dakin's reply in *Paul Elmer More,* pp. 238-40.

25. *Platonism* (Princeton, 1917), pp. viii-ix.

26. PEM to Robert Shafer, October 22, 1931.

27. PEM to Irving Babbitt, August 29, 1926.

28. *The Christ of the New Testament,* p. 5.

29. See, e.g., *The Catholic Faith* (Princeton, 1931), pp. 180-99.

Chapter Two

1. PEM to Erna Obermeier, April 11, 1935.

2. PEM to William Roscoe Thayer, October 2, 1911.

3. *Ibid.*

4. Daniel Aaron (ed.), *Paul Elmer More's Shelburne Essays on American Literature* (New York, 1963), includes most of More's collected essays on American writers; omitted are "Lafcadio Hearn," *SE,* II, 46-72; "Donald G. Mitchell," *SE,* V, 158-69; and "Modern Currents in American Literature," *NSE,* I, 53-76.

5. PEM to Alice More, September 1, 1888.

6. *Helena and Occasional Poems* (New York and London, 1890). The novels are *The Great Refusal* and *The Jessica Letters.*

7. Samuel Pendleton Cowardin, Jr., and Paul Elmer More, *The Study of English Literature* (New York, 1936), pp. 193-200. Whether or not More is the exclusive author of this passage, it states his opinion. Cowardin had begun the book while teaching at Princeton Preparatory School; More offered to read the manuscript, became interested in the work, and became a collaborator. The plan of the book was Cowardin's, and most of the writing too, although much of the latter was done or redone under More's direction. While More wanted the book to come out under Cowardin's name only, he admitted that it could not have appeared without his help; Cowardin maintained, although in this he was returning More's compliment, that the best paragraphs of the book were More's. PEM to Samuel P. Cowardin, Jr., February 29, 1936; the letter now bears marginal notations by

Cowardin. Which sections of *The Study of English Literature* were written by More would be hard to determine, but he subscribed to the entire doctrine of the book and expressed much of it in his other works.

8. See, e.g., More's discussion of Longfellow and Heine, *SE*, V, 135-38, and the essays "The Greek Anthology," *SE*, V, 1-21, and "Arthur Symons: The Two Illusions," *SE*, I, 122-46.

9. See *SE*, II, 172; "Ailing Fiction," New York *Evening Post*, October 8, 1904, p. 4; "The Novel and the Play," New York *Evening Post*, March 17, 1906, p. 4; *The Study of English Literature*, pp. 305-26.

10. New York *Evening Post*, March 17, 1906, p. 4.

11. PEM to Prosser Hall Frye, September 24, 1928.

12. PEM to Prosser Hall Frye, (probably) August, 1910.

13. PEM to Alice More, November 12, 1921.

14. PEM to Charles R. Lanman, August 1, 1903.

15. PEM to Percy H. Houston, December 3, 1923.

16. The Modern Library *Ulysses* reads "greatgrandfather" instead of "great-grandfather" and "wriggled" instead of "wriggling" (p. 114, the 1961 edition; p. 112, earlier editions).

17. "Children's Books," *Nation*, CI (December 2, 1915), 651.

18. "The Origins of Hawthorne and Poe," *SE*, I, 51-70; "George Crabbe," *SE*, II, 126-44; "Walt Whitman," *SE*, IV, 180-211; "Thoreau's Journal," *SE*, V, 106-31; "George Gissing," *SE*, V, 45-65; "Chesterfield," *SE*, V, 196-227; "Sir Thomas Browne," *SE*, VI, 154-86; "Jonathan Edwards," *SE*, XI, 35-65; "Henry Vaughan," *NSE*, I, 143-64; "How to Read Lycidas," *NSE*, III, 184-202.

Chapter Three

1. *"The Nation,"* writes Senator Paul H. Douglas, "under the editorship of Paul Elmer Moore [*sic*], had become a journal for highly-conservative professors of literature and seemed to be gasping out its last breath." *New Republic*, CL (March 21, 1964), 16.

2. The historical summary in this chapter is based chiefly on the following sources: Harold U. Faulkner, *The Quest for Social Justice, 1898-1914*, History of American Life Series, Vol. XI (New York, 1931). Ralph Henry Gabriel, *The Course of American Democratic Thought: An Intellectual History Since 1815* (New York, 1940). Eric Goldman, *Rendezvous With Destiny: A History of Modern American Reform* (New York, 1952). Richard Hofstadter, *Social Darwinism in American Thought, 1860-1915*, rev. ed. (Boston, 1955). Arthur Meier Schlesinger, *Political and Social Growth of the United States, 1852-1933*, rev. ed. (New York, 1936). Harvey Wish, *Society and Thought in Modern America: A Social and Intellectual History*

of the American People from 1865, Society and Thought in America,
Vol. II (New York, 1952).

3. The earliest of More's writings entirely given over to treating
some aspect of humanitarianism is "The Ancient Feud between
Philosophy and Art," *Atlantic Monthly,* LXXXVI (September, 1900),
337-47 (reprinted as "Tolstoy; or, The Ancient Feud between Philosophy and Art," *SE,* I, 193-224); *NSE,* III (1936), contains "Religion
and Social Discontent" (117-43) and "Church and Politics" (144-59).

4. *The Jessica Letters,* p. 55. Written in collaboration with Corra
May Harris, this novel consists of an exchange of letters between an
editor and a young woman reviewer. The editor's letters, from which
this quotation is taken, are More's contribution and they express his
own opinions on morality and public affairs.

5. PEM to Prosser Hall Frye, December 11, 1902.

6. Herbert W. Schneider, *A History of American Philosophy*
(New York, 1946), p. 534. See also Goldman, pp. 155-56.

7. Ralph Barton Perry, *The Thought and Character of William
James* (Boston, 1935), II, 521.

8. The following discussion of religious and economic fiction is
based on Charles H. Hopkins, *The Rise of the Social Gospel in
American Protestantism, 1865-1915* (New Haven, 1940), pp. 135-48;
Walter B. Rideout, *The Radical Novel in the United States, 1900-
1954: Some Interrelations of Literature and Society* (Cambridge,
Mass., 1956), pp. 12-58; Walter Fuller Taylor, *The Economic Novel in
America* (Chapel Hill, 1942), pp. 58-115.

9. Florence Converse, *The Burden of Christopher* (Boston, 1900),
p. 170. Ironically, this novel carries an epigraph, translated by Paul
Elmer More, from *Oedipus Tyrannus.* More had begun translating
that tragedy in 1898 but had never finished it; the excerpt Miss
Converse used might have been something he gave her during their
acquaintance at Shelburne, N. H., in 1899. See Dakin, *Paul Elmer
More,* pp. 65-67, 386.

10. "Tolstoy; or, The Ancient Feud between Philosophy and
Art," *SE,* I, 193-224; "Ailing Fiction," New York *Evening Post,* Octo-
ber 8. 1904, p. 4; "Whittier and After," New York *Evening Post,*
December 21, 1907, p. 4; *The Jessica Letters,* pp. 294-97.

11. Ernest Poole, *The Harbor* (New York, 1915), p. 377.

12. PEM to Louis T. More, March 9, 1908.

13. PEM to Louis T. More, May 24, 1912.

14. PEM to Louis T. More, February 25, 1917.

15. PEM to Alice More, June 15, 1916. See also PEM to Norman
Kemp Smith, April 27, 1916.

16. PEM to Louis T. More, October 15, 1918.

17. More did not approve of classical education in the United
States. He complained frequently of the philological emphasis in

what should be humanistic studies, and he worked both through his writings and through his personal influence to redeem them. See Dakin, *Paul Elmer More*, pp. 90-92 and 112-13, especially the list of More's articles on classical studies, pp. 90-91 n. 8.

18. See, e.g., Russell Kirk, *The Conservative Mind: From Burke to Santayana* (Chicago, 1953), pp. 377-86.

19. "Letters and Leadership," *Three Essays on America* (New York, 1934), p. 160.

20. *Independent*, LIII (May 30, 1901), 1263-64.

21. *Independent*, LIV (May 1, 1902), 1058-62.

22. PEM to Irving Babbitt, March 6, 1916.

23. Quoted in Dakin, *Paul Elmer More*, p. 367.

24. PEM to Mary Darrah More, December 12, 1921.

25. See *The Religion of Plato* (Princeton, 1921), pp. 294-95.

26. PEM to Louis T. More, April 11, 1936. For More's appreciation of the British character, see especially "The Lust of Empire," *Nation*, IC (October 22, 1914), 493-95, which contrasts the British and the Germans. Though it was reprinted as "The Philosophy of War," New York *Evening Post*, Saturday Supplement, October 24, 1914, p. 4, this essay should not be confused with "The Philosophy of the War," *SE*, IX, 221-43. Excerpts from "The Lust of Empire" are reprinted in Dakin, *A Paul Elmer More Miscellany*, pp. 58-61.

27. PEM to Robert Shafer, January 26, 1935. See also PEM to Seward B. Collins, January 20, 1935.

28. New York, 1955.

Chapter Four

1. All these volumes were published by the Princeton University Press; there was also a third edition of *Platonism* with a new Preface (Princeton, 1931) but otherwise not revised. In this chapter, I refer to these volumes in parenthetical citations using the following abbreviations: *P* for *Platonism* (I cite only the first edition), *RP* for *The Religion of Plato*, *HP* for *Hellenistic Philosophies*, *CNT* for *The Christ of the New Testament*, *CW* for *Christ the Word*, and *CF* for *The Catholic Faith*.

2. PEM to Louis T. More, April 9, 1920.

3. *homoousios*: of the same substance—from the clause in the Nicene Creed which states that the Son is of the same substance as the Father.

4. "The Spirit of Anglicanism," *Anglicanism: The Thought and Practice of the Church of England, Illustrated from the Religious Literature of the Seventeenth Century*, comp. and ed. Paul Elmer More and Frank Leslie Cross (London and Milwaukee, 1935), p. xxxii.

5. See Dakin, *Paul Elmer More*, p. 384.

6. *Anglicanism*, p. xxxi.

7. PEM to Alice More, November 8, 1918.
8. PEM to Marcus Selden Goldman, September 9, 1932.
9. "Interpretations of Plato," *Nation*, CVI (February 21, 1918), 210.
10. *Times Literary Supplement*, April 19, 1918, p. 192.
11. *Mind*, n. s., XXXI (October, 1922), 518-21; quotation, p. 521.
12. *Mind*, n. s., XXVII (January, 1919), 96-99; quotation, p. 96.
13. *Nation*, CVI (February 21, 1918), 209-10; quotations, p. 210.
14. *Platonism in Recent Religious Thought* (New York, 1958).
15. *Paul Elmer More*, p. 236.
16. *Aristotle and the Problem of Value* (Princeton, 1963), p. 26.
17. "Mr. More Discovers Christianity," *Sewanee Review*, XXXVI (April, 1928), 246-50; quotation, p. 248.
18. *Dublin Review*, CXCIII (July, 1933), 130-32; quotations, p. 130.
19. "Paul Elmer More," *Princeton Alumni Weekly*, XXXVII (February 5, 1937), 373.
20. PEM to Prosser Hall Frye, November 27, 1917.
21. Dakin, *Paul Elmer More*, p. 386.

Chapter Five

1. PEM to Paul G. Tomlinson, May 5, 1928.
2. *NSE*, III, 97-100; *The Study of English Literature*, pp. 383-84, 387-91.
3. *The Study of English Literature*, p. 390.
4. PEM to Brander Matthews, December 28, 1920.
5. PEM to Brander Matthews, December 18, 1921.
6. PEM to Robert Shafer, July 17, 1928. More disliked all three of the famous Jameses. In the father, he found "transcendentalism laid indecently bare" (PEM to Austin Warren, May 10, 1934); the trouble with the sons was that their father's sins had been visited upon them. The "fatuous atmosphere of his youth" prevented William from developing "into a sound as well as a brilliant philosopher," and it ruined young Henry altogether. At the time of these judgments, however, More apparently knew the elder Henry only through Austin Warren's *The Elder James* (PEM to Austin Warren, May 5, 1934).
7. PEM to Alice More, November 30, 1928.
8. More's relations with Eliot are discussed *passim* in Dakin, *Paul Elmer More*.
9. PEM to Philip S. Richards, October 12, 1930.
10. PEM to Erna Obermeier, January 28, 1935.
11. PEM to Prosser Hall Frye, September 8, 1931.
12. "The Cleft Eliot," *Saturday Review of Literature*, IX (November 12, 1932), 233, 235.

13. PEM to David Bowers, December 9, 1932.

14. PEM to Robert Shafer, October 8 and November 23, 1926.

15. PEM to Alice More, December 4, 1926.

16. PEM to Prosser Hall Frye, November 27, 1917.

17. PEM to Percy H. Houston, October 13, 1921.

18. PEM to William P. Trent, March 24, 1931. See also *The Jessica Letters*, p. 14.

19. More said on another occasion that he "rather admired" Frost's poetry. PEM to Alice More, March 10, 1921.

20. *Review*, II (April 17, 1920), 380-81.

21. *The Study of English Literature* names William Faulkner as "one of the most conspicuous" writers of a brutalized fiction which is less art than "clinical pathology," "a passing phase of exasperated nerves" (388). Since no corresponding remark appears in writings which are exclusively More's, it is possible that the opinion is Cowardin's.

22. In 1937 More believed that his prediction had already been fulfilled as it applied to Dreiser, Anderson, and Cabell; he gave Dos Passos an extension of "ten or fifteen years." "Marginalia, Part I," *American Review*, VIII (November, 1936), 12.

23. *The Rhetoric of Fiction* (Chicago, 1961), pp. 329-30. For *The Stranger*, see pp. 296-97. Also pertinent to More's moral objections to pure fiction is Booth's last chapter, "The Morality of Impersonal Narration" (pp. 377-98).

24. "Whittier and After," New York *Evening Post*, December 21, 1907, p. 4.

25. "Some Questions of Esthetics," *Transformations* (New York, 1926), p. 10.

26. PEM to Prosser Hall Frye, October 3, 1929.

27. See *SE*, II, 197-98, and J. Duncan Spaeth, "Conversations With Paul Elmer More," *Sewanee Review*, LI (October-December, 1943), 543.

28. *The Catholic Faith*, pp. 214-15.

29. In the following discussion I use the capitalized forms "Humanism" and "Humanist," either preceded or not by "New," to denote the principles and adherents of that movement in American criticism and "humanism" and "humanist" without capitals to identify the general principles for which More stood irrespective of their relation to any school. The distinction may be at times arbitrary.

30. Norman Foerster (ed.), *Humanism and America: Essays on the Outlook of Modern Civilization* (New York, 1930). C. Hartley Grattan (ed.), *The Critique of Humanism: A Symposium* (New York, 1930). Treatments of the critical debates of the 1920's and 1930's are given in Frederick J. Hoffman, *The Twenties: American Writing*

in the Postwar Decade, rev. ed. (New York, 1962), pp. 144-81; Alfred Kazin, *On Native Grounds: An Interpretation of Modern American Prose Literature* (New York, 1942), pp. 265-311; Robert E. Spiller, "The Battle of the Books," *Literary History of the United States: History,* 3rd ed., rev. (New York and London, 1963), pp. 1135-56; Willard Thorp, *American Writing in the Twentieth Century* (Cambridge, Mass., 1960), pp. 275-316; Morton Dauwen Zabel, "Introduction: Criticism in America," *Literary Opinion in America: Essays Illustrating the Status, Methods, and Problems of Criticism in the United States in the Twentieth Century,* 3rd ed., rev. (New York and Evanston, 1962), I, 1-43. Robert Shafer, *Paul Elmer More and American Criticism* (New Haven, 1935), studies its subject from the Humanist point of view.

31. See the criticisms of Eliot by Stanley P. Chase, pp. 223-25, and Gorham B. Munson, pp. 251-54.

32. PEM to Robert Shafer, April 1, 1930.

33. Excepting only Eliot, "and he, in spite of his genius, has long ceased to create," Rebecca West, e.g., referred to Foerster's contributors as "a league of the non-creative against the creative" which could inspire at best a literature of young men with Eliot's opinions but without his talent. "A Last London Letter—A Counterblast to Humanism," *Bookman,* LXXI (August 1930), 522.

34. *Writers on the Left: Episodes in American Literary Communism* (New York, 1961), p. 236.

35. PEM to George R. Elliott, March 31, 1929.

36. PEM to Robert Shafer, June 24, 1928.

37. PEM to Norman Foerster, February 4, 1929.

38. PEM to Prosser Hall Frye, January 19, 1930.

39. *Bookman,* LXXI (March, 1930), 1-11; reprinted in *NSE,* III, 1-24.

40. PEM to Robert Shafer, April 1, 1930.

41. PEM to Mary Darrah More, December 12, 1921.

42. PEM to Prosser Hall Frye, February 19, 1929.

43. PEM to George R. Elliott, July 28, 1929.

44. PEM to William P. Trent, March 24, 1931.

45. PEM to T. S. Eliot, March 24, 1931.

46. PEM to Prosser Hall Frye, June 19, 1929.

47. PEM to Robert Shafer, November 15, 1934.

Chapter Six

1. "Paul Elmer More," *Princeton Alumni Weekly,* XXXVII (February 5, 1937), 373.

2. "The Air of Quiet Study," New York *Evening Post,* August 17, 1912, p. 6.

3. "An Imaginary Conversation With Mr. P. E. More," *Americans* (New York, 1924), pp. 332-33.

4. October 2, 1911.

5. See, e.g., *SE*, X, 102 n, 255-56. Samuel C. Chew objects to More's modernization of Byron's punctuation in his edition of *The Complete Poetical Works of Lord Byron* (Boston and New York, 1905), preferring "the older style as more characteristic of Byron and his period." *The English Romantic Poets: A Review of Research,* ed. Ernest Bernbaum *et al.,* rev. ed. (New York, 1956), p. 143.

6. PEM to Percy H. Houston, July 6, 1926. George Lyman Kittredge, George Foot Moore, Roscoe Pound, and Babbitt were at Harvard.

7. The quotations are from George Steiner, "A Triumph of Insight," *Reporter*, XXVII (July 19, 1962), 54-56, a review of Sydney Freedberg, *Painting of the High Renaissance in Rome and Florence,* 2 vols. (Cambridge, Mass., 1962). Steiner contrasts the methods of Romantic and Victorian critics of art—Ruskin and Pater, e.g.—with those of modern formalist critics; what he says of Pater's method is, with certain reservations, true of More's.

8. See, in the *Shelburne Essays,* all pieces on American authors—most of them included in Daniel Aaron (ed.), *Paul Elmer More's Shelburne Essays on American Literature* (New York, 1963)—especially those on Thoreau, Hawthorne, Poe, and Emerson in *SE*, I; on Hawthorne in *SE*, II; on Whittier in *SE*, III; on Freneau, Thoreau, and Longfellow in *SE*, V; and on New England poetry, Edwards, Emerson, Norton, and Adams in *SE*, XI. See also "A Writer of New England," *Nation*, XCI (October 27, 1910), 386-87 (on Sarah Orne Jewett), and "A Note on Poe's Method," *NSE* I, 53-76 (reprinted in Aaron).

9. Poe's importance as a forerunner of symbolism, e.g., which More noted in 1935, was discussed in Edmund Wilson, *Axel's Castle: A Study of the Imaginative Literature of 1870-1930* (New York, 1931), p. 12.

10. *SE*, V, 117-18, a judgment confirmed by Henry A. Pochmann, *German Culture in America* (Madison, 1957), p. 434.

11. *The American Novel,* rev. ed. (New York, 1940), pp. 211-12.

12. "A Writer of New England," *Nation*, XCI (October 27, 1910), 386-87.

13. *The Power of Blackness: Hawthorne, Poe, Melville* (New York, 1958).

14. *The Cycle of American Literature* (New York, 1935), p. 12.

15. Baton Rouge, La., 1958.

16. H. L. Mencken, *Prejudices, Third Series* (New York, 1922), p. 178.

17. Frederick A. Pottle traces the decline of Shelley's reputation in the twentieth century to the influence of the New Humanists, and particularly to Babbitt's *Rousseau and Romanticism* (1919), but he notes that More's essay on Shelley (*SE*, VII, 1-26) anticipates Babbitt by about nine years. "The Case of Shelley," *English Romantic Poets*, ed. M. H. Abrams (New York, 1960), p. 194.

18. Levin, *The Power of Blackness*, p. 40. I have rearranged the elements in this quotation, which reads in the original, "the old assumption, which would not be seriously challenged today, that esthetics depends upon ethics."

19. Robert E. Spiller, *et al.*, *Literary History of the United States*: *History*, p. 1151.

Selected Bibliography

This bibliography makes no attempt to duplicate what is given in the Notes and References; it lists only More's most important works, some others which are likely to interest the general student, and a few bibliographical and biographical studies. The great number of his published writings would make any full listing of them impractical, even if all of them were known; while he has been the subject of numerous articles and is usually treated in histories of American literature and in general studies of the New Humanism, there are few full-length studies of him, most of these being unpublished masters' or doctoral theses. For a more complete listing both of his writings and of writings about him consult the footnotes and Bibliographical Note (p. 388) in Dakin, *Paul Elmer More*, and the Check Lists in Dakin, *A Paul Elmer More Miscellany*. The latter also lists other editions and printings of works named here.

PRIMARY SOURCES

A. Published Works

Anglicanism: The Thought and Practice of the Church of England, Illustrated from the Religious Literature of the Seventeenth Century. Comp. and ed. PAUL ELMER MORE and FRANK LESLIE CROSS. London: Society for Promoting Christian Knowledge, 1935. Contains, as an introduction, More's essay, "The Spirit of Anglicanism."

Aristocracy and Justice: Shelburne Essays, Ninth Series. Boston and New York: Houghton Mifflin, 1915. Essays on politics and society.

The Catholic Faith. Complementary Volume to *The Greek Tradition.* Princeton: Princeton University Press, 1931.

A Century of Indian Epigrams: Chiefly from the Sanskrit of Bhartrihari. Boston and New York: Houghton Mifflin, 1898.

The Christ of the New Testament. The Greek Tradition. Vol. III. Princeton: Princeton University Press, 1924.

Christ the Word. The Greek Tradition. Vol. IV. Princeton: Princeton University Press, 1927.

The Demon of the Absolute. New Shelburne Essays, Vol. I. Princeton: Princeton University Press, 1928.

The Drift of Romanticism: Shelburne Essays, Eighth Series. Boston and New York: Houghton Mifflin, 1913.

The Great Refusal: Being Letters of a Dreamer in Gotham. Ed. PAUL ELMER MORE. Boston and New York: Houghton Mifflin, 1894. A novel written by More.

Helena and Occasional Poems. New York and London: G. P. Putnam's Sons, 1890.

Hellenistic Philosophies. The Greek Tradition. Vol. II. Princeton: Princeton University Press, 1923.

The Jessica Letters: An Editor's Romance. New York and London: G. P. Putman's Sons, 1904. A novel published anonymously by Paul Elmer More and Corra May Harris.

"Marginalia, Part I." *American Review,* VIII (November, 1936), 1-30. Reminiscences.

A New England Group and Others: Shelburne Essays, Eleventh Series. Boston and New York: Houghton Mifflin, 1921.

On Being Human. New Shelburne Essays. Vol. III. Princeton: Princeton University Press, 1936.

Pages from an Oxford Diary. Princeton: Princeton University Press, 1937. Meditations on religion and philosophy, ostensibly of an Oxford don.

Paul Elmer More's Shelburne Essays on American Literature. Ed. DANIEL AARON. New York: Harcourt, Brace and World, 1963. The only collection of More's literary essays now in print.

Platonism. Princeton: Princeton University Press, 1917. A second edition, revised (Princeton, 1926), became the Introductory Volume to *The Greek Tradition,* but incorporates no significant changes. A third edition (Princeton, 1931) contains a new preface but does not otherwise differ from the second.

The Religion of Plato. The Greek Tradition. Vol. I. Princeton: Princeton University Press, 1921.

The Sceptical Approach to Religion. New Shelburne Essays. Vol. II. Princeton: Princeton University Press, 1934.

Selected Shelburne Essays. World's Classics, No. 434. Oxford and New York: Oxford University Press, 1935. More's own selection from the *Shelburne Essays.*

Shelburne Essays, First Series. New Edition. Boston and New York: Houghton Mifflin, 1904.

Shelburne Essays, Second Series. New Edition. Boston and New York: Houghton Mifflin, 1905.

Shelburne Essays, Third Series. New Edition. Boston and New York: Houghton Mifflin, 1905.

Shelburne Essays, Fourth Series. New Edition. Boston and New York: Houghton Mifflin, 1906.

Shelburne Essays, Fifth Series. New York and London: G. P. Putnam's Sons, 1908.

Shelburne Essays, Sixth Series: Studies of Religious Dualism. New
Edition. Boston and New York: Houghton Mifflin, 1909.
Shelburne Essays, Seventh Series. New Edition. Boston and New York:
Houghton Mifflin, 1910.
The Study of English Literature. By SAMUEL PENDLETON COWARDIN,
JR., and PAUL ELMER MORE. New York: Henry Holt, 1936.
With the Wits: Shelburne Essays, Tenth Series. Boston and New York:
Houghton Mifflin, 1919.

B. *Letters*

Originals or copies of the letters used in this book are now de-
posited in the Princeton University Library; many of them are reprinted, either fully or in part, in Dakin, *Paul Elmer More.*

SECONDARY SOURCES

DAKIN, ARTHUR HAZARD. *Paul Elmer More.* Princeton: Princeton
University Press, 1960. A biography containing generous ex-
cerpts from More's correspondence.
————. *A Paul Elmer More Miscellany.* Portland, Me.: Anthoensen
Press, 1950. Contains selections from More's uncollected essays,
selections from writings attributed to him, a Check List of his
works, and a Check List of works about him.
HANFORD, JAMES HOLLY. "The Paul Elmer More Papers," *Princeton
University Library Chronicle,* XXII (Summer 1961), 163-68.
Describes Princeton's holdings of letters, literary manuscripts, and
notebooks.
SHAFER, ROBERT. *Paul Elmer More and American Criticism.* New
Haven: Yale University Press, 1935. A biographical-critical study
by one of the New Humanists.

Index

Index